MY BEST BOSS EVER

A Collection of Stories

How the best bosses earned the trust, respect and admiration of their employees for a lifetime.

Rory Rowland

1

Copyright

Table of Contents

3

Acknowledgments

I would like to dedicate this effort: to my wife, Tedi, who has always given me the best advice and more loving support than I deserve, and to my children, Eliot, Josh, Michaela and J.P. who bring joy to life.

To my father, Robert, who has always been a dreamer; from him I caught the flame.

I would also like to acknowledge help from the following people: Quentin Templeton for listening to the interviews and his skill at putting them on paper; my children, Eliot, Michaela and Josh for their review and ideas; and as always, my wife, Tedi, who was my best source of support, help and shrewd manuscript assessment.

Share with Me

I would love to hear from you! This book could not have been completed without the help of hundreds of individuals who took the time to share the stories of their best boss ever. I know that the next book will be even better, simply because you will add your story to it.

I invite you to tell me how this book has affected you and changed the way you think about leadership. Please tell me what you would like to see more or less of, and which story was your favorite. While you are at it, do not hesitate to tell me *your* best boss story!

You can write, call, or even email me your best boss story and submit it for consideration in the next "My Best Boss Ever" book.

In addition to your best boss, I would like to hear about your best:
- Coach
- Service
- Teacher
- Salesperson
- Manager
- Meeting
- Soldier
- CEO

Or, any other idea you may have about the BEST you have received!

Write us and send your submissions to:

> Rory Rowland
> 14401 Covington Rd.
> Independence, MO 64055
>
> Phone: 816-478-3249
> Email: rrr3@ix.netcom.com

You can also submit a story or send an email by visiting my website at roryrowland.com.

Introduction

Management is the winner's edge in any successful business. The book "My Best Boss Ever" takes the fundamental lessons from the best bosses and encapsulates those lessons in many different (story) chapters.

To develop this book, I talked to hundreds of employees and asked them this simple question, "Who is the best boss you ever worked for and why?" The results and lessons I have learned from these discussions led me to the following key lessons for managers: care and concern for the employee, mentoring, knowing the hopes, wishes, dreams and aspirations of your employees and one of the most important lessons of all, leaving a legacy. The best bosses did not rely on manipulation or psychology in their "bag of tricks." They held an uncommon ability to build relationships and an overwhelming belief in their employees. These best bosses had a commitment to be a good manager but to also be a mentor. These best managers also possessed the ability to identify and find solutions to help the employees become the best they could be. The best bosses went far beyond enforcement of the rules to empowering the employee to live a better life.

"My Best Boss Ever" outlines a series of powerful tools the best bosses used to become the best boss ever. The interviews I conducted give several different slants on the important tools managers use to improve the performance and character of employees in *any* organization.

The stories included in "My Best Boss Ever" are from my conferences. These stories reveal universal truths of what makes the best bosses. The stories of the masters included in this book will help managers and leaders for years to come and will help rookie managers get a head start on what are the important keys of being a successful manager.

Pick the Weeds

"We learn by example and by direct experience because there are real limits to the adequacy of verbal instruction."
Malcolm Gladwell

My best boss ever was J. Willard Marriott Jr.

I used to be a regional manager for the Marriott Corporation and on occasion, J. Willard Marriott Jr. would visit my region to survey his hotels. He came to one of the hotels in the south, and it was a warm, beautiful day in spring. It was the kind of day that makes you wish you were young again.

As we approached the hotel, the manager of the property came out to greet Mr. Marriott and myself. After exchanging pleasantries, we walked into the hotel. We passed by a flower patch that unfortunately had some weeds in it. Mr. Marriott got on his hands and knees and began to pull the weeds.

I had worked with Mr. Marriott enough to know to get down and help. Unfortunately, the manager stood there and simply watched us. Noticing this, I got up, placed my hands on his shoulders, and applied a little pressure. He caught on and got down on his hands and knees with us. The three of us finished the job.

Mr. Marriott did not say anything that day, but he spoke volumes. If you see weeds, pick them. People will get the idea.

Even though Mr. Marriott never said anything else about it, on subsequent visits to this hotel, I never, ever saw weeds in the flowerbed again. Never.

See the Potential
Larry Kemball

"You can't wait for inspiration. You have to go after it..."
Jack London

Ewing Kauffman was an excellent speaker and motivator. He was having a sales meeting for the company, and was getting everyone fired up. We were ready to take on the world. We could have run through walls, he was simply excellent at getting everyone focused and fired up. During his speech he asked everyone to take out their business cards and write down the percentage they would be over quota for the year. He did not ask us to write down a goal. He asked us 'what percentage you would be over quota?' I took out my card because I was so fired up, and wrote down a ridiculous number. Everyone else did the same thing, we all wrote down numbers that were nothing short of crazy.

At the end of the meeting, he stood at the door and he shook our hands and collected the cards. Collectively, everyone said, 'oops.' Everyone knew they were had. Then every month we would get a memo personally from 'Mr. K' as we affectionately called him. The memo reminded us how we were doing. If we were ahead of quota, he would tell us what a great job we were doing, and if we were behind, he would encourage us to do more. Everyone in the company realized what he had done, and we all talked about it after the meeting and during the entire year. We all agreed it was a great leadership moment.

What did it do for the company and me?

It was the best year I ever had up to that point, and it was the best year for the company up to that point. It taught me the power of written goals, and the power of peer pressure. He made all of us better. He made all of us push beyond our perceived limits. That is the secret of a best boss. Best bosses make all of us better. Ewing Kauffman made me reach for the best of myself. In addition, he had a way of getting it, and more.

Editor's Note:

Ewing Kauffman was the prototypical entrepreneur, who started with few resources, grew his firm into a multibillion-dollar company over four decades, and did so in an ethical and compassionate manner. His company, Marion Laboratories, was later purchased by Merrill Dow, and he was the original owner of the Kansas City Royals.

Manage by M&M's®
Carolyn Warden

"The conventional definition of management is getting work done through people, but real management is developing people through work."
Agha Hasan Abedi

My best boss managed by using the power of M&M's®.

Remember that first job and the pressure you felt.

You always had to hurry with the constant effort to work fast because of your lack of knowledge. The hurried feeling that never seemed to go away those first few days—always having to rush around in a helter-skelter fashion because you did not know it all, yet.

When you are at the ticket booth you see customers standing, waiting in line, looking at you and then you read their minds, "Oh this is the rookie, they have no idea what they are doing and we ended up in their line." Then, you do some more mind reading and they go on further, "Why don't they get someone out here that knows what they are doing?" The feeling of stress, anxiety and panic just grows. Then magically another employee appears in the ticket booth next to you and they clear the line in no time, with what looked like little or no effort. You experience the humiliation of not being that skilled in processing tickets and the first time in your life feeling a

14

stress your parents cannot fix. Then an employee that was never very friendly says, "When are you ever going to learn this stuff? It's easy." The feelings of inadequacy jump out to grab you like a monster at a haunted house. When the stress would pile up and the feeling of inadequacy would rise up like an insurrection, I would go talk to my best boss ever.

If I had a problem and I went to talk to her about it, she would invite me to sit down and invite me to enjoy some of the M&M's® that were always in a bowl at her desk.

Of course, I would pop some M&M's® in my mouth. She would excuse herself, because at that moment she always seemed to have to make a short phone call. To this day, I really do not know if she was actually making a phone call. She could have been calling time and temperature, for all I know. However, those few moments allowed me to get a bit of a sugar rush and a moment for myself to relax. Her office was a safe place, a place where I could go to be heard. After eating a few M&M's® and taking in some relaxing air, even though I did not realize at the moment the importance of just sitting there and breathing, nothing seemed quite so challenging. After she concluded her phone call, she would give me her full attention and then I could tell her anything that was on my mind. Her listening skills were legendary with everyone who worked on the boat. I did not go to her office to talk, I always went to her office to be heard. Being heard is much different from being allowed to talk. She always listened so intently, in a non-judgmental way and after the M&M's® and a few moments of being heard, I was always able to go back out there and give it another try. She did not just seem to listen; she seemed to really give me a second chance. After talking with her, I felt refreshed, invigorated and recharged, and ready to try again.

Therefore, the power of this best manager was that she always had something to give us. Although supplying the colorful and tasty M&M's®, her best skill was her ability to listen to us regardless of what we had to say. Because she was such a great listener, she was able to allow us to talk through it and she only asked clarifying questions. This allowed me to hear myself and I presented the opportunity to correct myself. I did not realize the power of this technique until much later in life. I was always grateful that she listened, but I was more grateful that she taught me how to be a great boss. I still to this day keep in touch with her. Her skills and abilities made an impression that lasted a lifetime.

Respect
Roy Crawford

My best boss was General John Shalikashvili, Former Chairman of the Joint Chiefs of Staff. He was born in Poland and worked his way from an enlisted private to the rank of four-star general. He would often tell me that he learned his English from watching John Wayne movies after school.

At the time, he was a two star general in commanding the 1st Battalion, 84th Field Artillery, and 9th Infantry Division at Fort Lewis. He was not only extremely intelligent and knew everything that was going on, he also cared about people and treated everyone with respect, regardless of rank. That made him my best boss.

We were dealing with the forest fires in Yellowstone National Park in 1988 and had to send a brigade to help. When they were to return, a young man decided that he wanted to have some of the equipment that was loaned to him by the government. He placed lanterns and other supplies in his own personal trunk to be sent back.

When he returned to base, someone had noticed the missing items and reported it. He was a warrant officer, so the authority to deliver punishment was reserved for the division commander, General Shalikashvili. I was on the secretary general's staff at that time and literally

17

sat inches from his office door. When the young man came in, I recognized him as one of my Sunday school students. He asked if I knew why he was there, and he was obviously embarrassed when I said, yes.

He explained his discomfort in facing the division commander, and I replied that he should not worry. I described how the general was a fair man and would treat anyone with respect.

When he came out some time later, he told me that I was right. "He did punish me, but he treated me with respect. He listened to my side of the story, got all the facts, and explained what I did was wrong. But he also described what I could do to save my career."

The young officer could have been chewed out for stealing from the government, but General Shalikashvili took the time to explain what he could do better next time. He treated everyone with respect, even people who did something wrong.

As a leader, you have to be able to put emotion aside when you are disciplining someone. General Shalikashvili's ability to coach while disciplining is probably his greatest trait.

Getting the Credit I Didn't Earn
Bill Cowles

*"Giving credit where credit is due is a very rewarding
habit to form. Its rewards are inestimable."*
Loretta Young

I was 16 and the third string center on the varsity high school football team. This meant that the cheerleaders had a better chance of playing than I did. Nevertheless, being on the team was important to my social status in high school.

One day between classes, the principal stopped me in the hallway and said the local newspaper was looking for a sportswriter, mostly to cover high school games on weekends. He knew that I had my own car and also knew that I had built a reputation as a strong writer. I was not sure how to respond, so tried to duck the answer by saying, "Well, we're in the middle of football season. I'll have to talk to coach."

The principal looked me in the eye and said, "I've already talked to coach. It's OK with him." My football career had been decided for me.

So, after cleaning out my locker, my next stop was the local newspaper office to unravel the mystery of journalism and to unleash my talents on this new opportunity.

My first meeting with the Sports Editor was on a Friday afternoon. He was the prototypical reporter—overweight, unshaven, chain-smoking and no-nonsense. His desk was strewn with paper. Clutter and chaos seemed to be the forces that held the place together.

He did not have time for many pleasantries after hello, and we dove right into the operations of the cumbersome Graflex Speed Graphic camera, slides and battery pack I would have to tote along the sidelines. A clipboard loaded with yellow copy paper was easy to handle, but the prize awaiting my first assignment was my very own Press Card. Here was my ticket to the big-time. I now had access to the sidelines. Front-row seats wherever I went. The smell of a sweat-soaked football helmet and the cramping of interminable bus rides were but distant wistful memories.

My first journalistic assignment was to cover a game between two local high school rivals. Off I went, camera, clipboard and Press Card prominently displayed. I took as many photos as I could; spelled players' names as best I could; recorded the events and comments of the players and coaches as best I could. I had no idea what journalism was supposed to be like, so I reasoned that volume was a good start.

After the game, I hauled my bounty back to the newspaper as fast as I could, but it was still well after 10 p.m. by the time I got there. Still learning the ropes, I was shown where to deposit the camera for film developing, and then where to sit and write my story.

Eagerly, I grabbed pencil and paper and began writing the account of that epic battle between two gridiron giants who showed no quarter and.... Suddenly, by my shoulder, the Sports Editor loomed and boomed, "What the heck are you doing?"

"Writing my story," I said. He scooped up my copy paper and pencils and threw them into the trashcan and, in the same motion, deposited a well-worn Smith-Corona in front of me.

"Journalists type," he said matter-of-factly.

"But, I don't know how to type," I weakly protested.

"Tonight, you learn," was all he said on his way back to his own desk pile.

As arguing didn't seem advisable, I began hunting and pecking and re-hunting and re-pecking to the point where I had amassed about a page and a half of readable copy—and it took only to 3 a.m.! Proudly, I handed it in.

After a quick look, the Editor said: "That will do. Go home and get some sleep."

Of course, I slept past noon that Saturday and, when I finally awoke, I ran outside to grab the paper from its afternoon delivery.

And, there it was—on the first page of the Sports section—a picture that I took and a three-column story underneath it that touted: *by Bill Cowles, Sports Reporter.*

I read that story in record time. Then I went back and read it slowly, savoring the language—the powerful adjectives, the vivid metaphors, and the colorful descriptions. I read it a third time when I finally realized that not a word of the article was mine. NOT A WORD. My version was so bad that he had to rewrite the entire story. Still, he put my byline on it. Moreover, he and I were the only ones who knew. He never told anyone.

I worked for him for two years. He wrote me a recommendation letter for college. He sponsored me in a local writing competition. He furnished much of the editorial material for the paper when I won that competition. He wrote job recommendations for me after I graduated from college.

He was the best boss I ever had because he was one of the wisest people I have ever known. He knew what I had given up to work for him. He knew that I did not know anything about his craft. He knew that I would work hard. He knew that I would learn more from getting the credit for a great story I did not write, than from suffering the ridicule and blame for a bad story I did write.

He taught me to be a pretty good writer, and he taught me how to work with people. Give the

22

credit; take the blame—skills that have helped me for a lifetime.

Reset to Zero

"Anger is a great force. If you control it, it can be
transmuted into a power
which can move the whole world."
William Shenstone

As a child, you know to ask your parents for a favor at precisely the right moment.

Timing is everything.

You would never ask your parents for a new bike immediately after they had a big fight. You would wait for that precise moment when the world and the stars were in proper alignment. The same is true for bosses. That is why my boss is the best boss ever.

One day, I needed to talk to my boss about an important challenge I was having. As I approached the office, the door was slightly ajar. Slowly approaching, I realized that a co-worker was being reprimanded for some errors he had made earlier in the week. Out of respect, I stepped back far enough so that I could not hear what was being said. I considered leaving, but the problem was urgent. The days of my childhood came racing back as I considered leaving. I could wait until later, not knowing what could happen if I asked now. I did not want to face the Pandora's box that was unleashed by another employee. Just as I was calculating my options, out walked the reprimanded employee, followed by my boss!

My boss saw me and invited me in, so I was obviously faced with an immediate decision. I quickly thought, "Do I go in and face the wrath left over, or do I select the better part of valor, turn on my heels and go back to my cubicle?" However, before I could make a decision, my boss had flashed that famous smile, and invited me into her office and asked how she could help me.

My fear and dread vanished as I realized that there was not an ounce of anger left over. The amazing thing was, she did not even appear to be angry at all. I thought, "How in the world did her anger vanish so quickly?" I could simply not understand how someone could be so frustrated one moment and perfectly calm and congenial the next. To be honest, I had never seen behavior like this before from anyone, much less in a boss. Typically, I saw bosses who, once they were angry, would remain that way and word quickly spread to stay out of their way.

However, my boss helped answer my question, gave me some great suggestions and wished me well. I left her office with my fear lifted, but still questioning how she got rid of anger so quickly.

Over the next few weeks, I pondered what she had done. She had displayed some amazing self-control and focus. About a month later, I finally mustered up the courage to ask how the feat was accomplished. She quietly responded, "Reset to zero." She said that she had learned the technique the hard way, after getting angry with the wrong employee in the past. She told me, "One day, my anger simmered over to another employee who was not involved in the problem. She ended up getting the brunt of my anger, even though she was not involved at all. My anger and frustration left her in tears and she packed up her things and quit on the spot. As a boss, I was devastated. I promised I would never direct my anger at the wrong individual again."

She then explained to me how she learned the concept of "reset to zero." She was working on her computer when it suddenly froze. After calling the IT help line, to see what could be done, they instructed her to reboot. The IT technician responded, "When the computer gets overwhelmed, sometimes we have to reboot and it resets everything to zero." She thought about it, realized the power and understood she quickly had to implement it into her life.

By asking my boss what reset to zero meant, I learned a valuable lesson on management and life. I learned that, sometimes we all have to reset to zero when our anger gets the best of us and we get overwhelmed.

Be a Backstop

*"Character is power; it makes friends, draws patronage
and support and opens the way to wealth, honor and
happiness."*
John Howe

She just continued to scream at me.

The people in the hallway stopped. They looked in, they stared, my nerves continued to become more unraveled the more she yelled. All the children in the hallway outside my office got quiet—very quiet. They just looked at this mother scream as her shrill voice continued to escalate.

Imagine your worst, most irate customer—ever. You wish you had a vanish button, or you wish she was standing over a trap door. Suddenly your daydreams are interrupted by the harsh sound of reality, her shrill voice neither stops nor goes away. She just continues to scream at you. Her anger continues to grow as you do everything possible to calm her. Nothing works; no suggestion makes any difference. She just continues to get madder and madder.

Since I am the secretary, I cannot fix her problem. It is so large even the principal of the grade school cannot fix it. I try to politely inform her of that, to no avail. She is just out of control and no one can stop her. Her anger finally gets the best of her and as she storms toward the doors and as she passes the other side, she yells, "I am going to central

27

office and I will have your job." She is gone, but not forgotten, as the situation loomed in my mind for days.

In our school district when a parent goes to central office, many times it meant you could go ahead and pack your bags because your career with the school district was over. The fear and dread of her going to central office continued to build all day long. Then the inevitable e-mail appeared. It was from the school district superintendent asking me to come to his office. Thankfully, a carbon copy was sent to my principal.

My principal called me into her office to ask about the situation. She listened carefully to my side of the story and after hearing it, realized there was no simple or easy solution for this parent. My principal informed me to not worry about it. She even stated that she would go to central office on my behalf. She went and dealt with the anger of the superintendent and the angry parent. The feeling of relief for working for a boss who was a backstop was incredible.

Of course, the story became legendary at our school. Our principal's reputation and admiration from all the staff grew by leaps and bounds with this one event.

The best thing I liked about my best boss was that she was a backstop for any challenges or problems that arose. I would have walked through fire for her, because she was there for me, even when I thought I might lose my job at the district.

Invest in Growth

*"Quality questions create a quality life. Successful people
ask better questions, and as a result,
they get better answers."*

Anthony Robbins

I was seventeen when I got my first real job. I had the prestigious title of "Lab Technician," but I am sure that was just for funding purposes. In reality, I just drove a truck all day. Regardless, I was happy to have a job and years later, I am happy I had the best boss ever as my first boss.

My first week on the loading dock, my boss—Jack—came up and said, "Every week, I take a fifteen minute walk with all of my employees and I'd like to set up your time for every Friday." Being so young, I was not entirely sure if this was normal for a boss to take time out of his busy day, but I was not going to refuse his request. Before walking away, Jack made direct eye contact and said, "Every week during our walk, I want to learn something from you about your job. So as you work, think about what has helped you become more efficient and what has not. Then we will just talk about it."

As he walked away, I brushed off the chat as some new program that would soon fizzle, probably before Friday even came. However, right on schedule, Jack walked up to me on Friday and asked, "Are you ready for our walk?" We set off together and after some small talk about home,

Jack proposed, "What has worked well for you this week?" As I started to explain everything I had learned about my new job, I could tell that Jack already knew most of what I had to say. Suddenly though, Jack exclaimed, "Wow! That is a great idea! I want you to share that with the team."

Fear suddenly engulfed me. Everyone I knew at work had a PhD after their name, was a scientist, or triple my age--sometimes all three. I tried to back out, respectfully, but Jack insisted. For the rest of our walk, Jack coached me on how to organize my ideas and present them to the group. He even assured me that he would be by my side for the whole presentation, if I should need him. In just a short walk, Jack not only helped me respect my own opinion, he also taught me that I had ideas to share and that those ideas had value.

By simply asking what had gone well for me that week, he changed the course of my entire life. He helped me recognize the value of my ideas and I learned to see things from a different perspective. I now know that in every situation we are in, we need to continue to grow and learn. Despite your credentials behind your name, you can always learn more. I respected Jack because he not only respected me, but he also respected my ideas, my opinions and he made me feel important, significant and even valuable. All while I was only seventeen.

Like a Son
Rick Olson

"You don't raise heroes, you raise sons. And if you treat them like sons, they'll turn out to be heroes, even if it's just in your own eyes."
Walter M. Schirra, Sr.

In 1975, I was just out of college looking for a ministry job. I applied at First Assembly Church in Rockford, Illinois. The Reverend Ernie Moen was pastor. My first day on the job was a Saturday evening. There were people camped out all over the church property and there were kids in activities everywhere. I soon realized it was the annual church campout weekend. The Reverend Ernie Moen was a master of bringing people together, which was evident through the mixture of fellowship, worship and fun. With all the activity going on, Ernie invited me into his office for a brief interview.

In his office, he cast for me a vision of what it would be like if I worked there—at the time the church was 2000 members strong. Ernie was a big thinker and he was offering me the opportunity to be the youth minister with approximately five students involved in the youth program—but he obviously wanted to see it grow. He set out two simple rules, number one, 'keep it biblical,' and number two, 'cover his back.' Very simple instructions; follow the Bible and no surprises. Other than those two rules, Ernie said that if I wanted to take the kids around the world,

I should go for it. That was Ernie's way: simple rules with a big vision.

With Ernie's help and support, we started with the foundation of those five kids and after five years, we exploded to 250. The great thing about Ernie was he never hogged the praise and he was always more than willing to share the glory. His public praise was one of his best strengths and he used that praise as a great motivator.

His other strength was his ability to tap into your creativity. He was always working at expanding your thinking. I had never dreamed I would be given the responsibility or freedom that he gave me. However, he was a master at casting a vision of how he wanted the organization to grow. He truly wanted to bring the message of Jesus to everyone in the community. He was no micromanager, he did not stand over your shoulder, he was true to his word, keep it biblical and keep him informed.

With his help, support and trust we took a group of kids around the world, a journey I will never forget. However, the most important journey he led me on, was the ability to find the leader in myself. He encouraged me to expand my thinking in so many areas.

After five years, I resigned to move on to another position at another church; I received the biggest surprise of all. He read a poem from the pulpit to the entire congregation. He had three marvelous daughters, but no son, so his poem was titled "If I had a son." He went on to say that if he had a son he would want him to be just like me! Here I was leaving a job and he made me feel like I was leaving home.

That day I was on cloud nine to have him share that poem with the entire congregation. It was a "wow" moment in my life. Ernie's real power was his ability to always make me feel like a million bucks; and to help me believe I could do more than I thought was possible. Because of him, my belief in myself was greatly expanded. After working with Ernie I was no longer a kid right out of college, I was a young man, with huge possibilities.

For that new vision of myself, I will always be grateful.

Be Supportive
David J. Mervin

*"To get rich never risk your health.
Health is the wealth of wealth."*

Richard Baker

The best boss I ever had, Bill Jaeger, had human empathy; he created a team spirit and he was animated and kind, but incredibly focused. He was driven by success, but he wanted us to be successful too.

I had just received the position of Vice President in my company four months back. The expectations and responsibilities were massive, to say the least. I came home one night to learn that my wife had been diagnosed with cancer. I knew that the industry was too fast paced to take off weeks, much less months at a time, so I went in to talk to the owner of the company about my resignation.

As I walked in, he could obviously see the turmoil on my face. I told him that my wife was diagnosed with cancer and would undergo treatment soon. He clearly felt my grief. He asked how my wife and I were doing and I simply said, "Scared to death." He listened to me tell him what was going on, the prognosis and the plan of action. Finally, I offered him my resignation, to not prevent the company from suffering. He looked me in the eye and said, "You go take care of your family and

35

when your wife gets healthy, you come back. Your job will be here."

I would have worked for the company for nothing after that.

I went home and told my wife the news and she started to cry, knowing that we belong to a corporate family that was willing to be there and be a support system for us. The knowledge that we had that kind of support from my company made everything easier.

My wife went through the treatments and the surgery in flying colors. True to their word, the company welcomed me warmly after it was all said and done.

Find the Funding

*"In helping others, we shall help ourselves, for whatever good
we give out completes the circle and comes back to us."*
Flora Edwards

The best boss I ever had was while I was in college.
I worked my way through school on a work-study
program. My boss had many likable traits, but two
reasons stand above the rest. First off, he held a
very flexible schedule for me. This allowed me to
easily work around my class schedule. The second
reason was that he understood my incredible desire
to finish my college degree. He did not just see me
as an employee, but as a person working to be
better.

During my senior year, the work-study program ran
out of funding. I immediately began to have fears
about how I was going to pay for college. My boss
called me into his office and informed me that the
funding may soon run out, but that he would see
what we could do. With this one initiative, he
started applying for grants to allow me to fund my
college education. He was successful in attaining the
necessary funds and I was able to complete my
education.

I will always be grateful for my boss, who took an
interest in me. The initiative he took enabled me to
finish my education and go on to become successful.
My sense of gratefulness will never be extinguished.
Because of his influence, my life was improved
forever.

Hopes, Dreams, Wishes and Aspirations
Rory Rowland

"Our life is composed greatly from dreams, from the unconscious, and they must be brought into connection with action. They must be woven together."

Anais Nin

In the late 90s when I was brand-new to the speaking business, a client arranged for a limousine to pick me up at the airport. It was the first time I had ever had a limousine pick me up while on business. My sense of self-importance was incredible, however that feeling of self-importance was to be overshadowed by what I was about to learn. Rosie was the limousine driver who was to take me from the airport to the World Center Marriott in Orlando, Florida. Rosie was happy, friendly, and quick with a story. Since this is the first time a client had ever had a limousine for me to get from the airport, I really did not know the protocol. Rosie guided me to the limousine and just at the right moment, she held the back limousine door open so I could step inside. Coming from a blue-collar family, I asked if I could just sit up front with her. My father was a truck driver, so obviously I did not know anything about riding in the back of limousines. She smiled and quickly moved to open up the front door for me to climb into.

While upfront, I asked her how she liked being a limousine driver and how she liked working for the World Center Marriott. She said she loved it and would gladly work there for many years. She said that the World Center Marriott was special because the General Manager was extraordinary. The General Manager, she said, knew almost all the employees by their first name. He had also given many of them a nickname. I asked Rosie what her nickname was and she responded with, "Trouble." Her response showed that smile again and a bit of a laugh. Her sense of pride that she was recognized as important was very evident.

During my stay, I asked other employees how long they had worked there and if they liked it there. They all said yes, with a smile and enthusiasm. I could not find anyone who had worked there for less than five years! For the service industry, in my mind, that was extraordinary. Particularly in Orlando, where an employee can leave one job and get another the same day.

After my speaking engagement at the World Center Marriott, Rosie took me in the limousine, (notice I was again in a limousine) and I told her about the extraordinary service I received at the hotel and what a great job they did there. I then asked her to tell me a story that illustrated the General Manager's extraordinary skills. Rosie shared a story about a housekeeper who always wanted to see Bill Cosby perform. However, since she was a housekeeper in Orlando, Florida, it was difficult for her to travel to Las Vegas. On top of that, the show tickets would be too expensive. Since the General Manager was so people-oriented, he knew and remembered many details about his employees.

When Bill Cosby was scheduled to perform in a corporate event in Orlando, the general manager remembered this fact. On his own accord, he contacted Bill Cosby's manager and asked if the housekeeper could meet Bill Cosby and then possibly see his show. Bill Cosby's folks were incredibly gracious and not only did they allow her to meet Bill Cosby, but they gave her backstage passes, she had her picture taken with him and she was able to watch the performance with the other folks who were at the corporate event.

Rosie told me that the housekeeper thanked the General Manager profusely for allowing her to live a life long dream.

The General Manager knew the hopes, wishes, dreams and aspirations of his employees. He used that knowledge to deepen and strengthen his relationships with his employees. Moreover, that knowledge helped him earn the respect, admiration and loyalty of his employees for a lifetime.

In the Loop

"A well-informed mind is the best security against the contagion of folly and of vice."
Ann Radcliffe

My best boss ever kept us in the loop of what was going on at the bank.

At the time, I was working for a large regional bank in southern Florida. I had been working there for about ten years and had a big portion of my career invested in that bank. One day, I began to hear some rumors that we might be in trouble. Of course, my antenna went up and I began to research a little further. Shortly after my research began, a memo circulated that asked all of the employees to attend a mandatory meeting at a local hotel. About 600 employees attended. There were no balloons, no festive decorations and no semblance of any celebration at this event.

After everyone was seated, the doors were closed and the CEO took the podium at the center of the stage. He shared with us the shocking news that the bank was in serious financial trouble. He asked us to keep this information extremely confidential. He asked us not to even share this information with our spouses or parents. He said if we did, it might cause a run on the bank and cause all of us to lose our jobs immediately. He went on further to explain that we would have career counselors available to help any employees' transition to new jobs. For those employees who

41

stayed up to the point of liquidation or merger, a severance package would be provided. He said that although his goal was two-fold, he first wanted to make sure that we heard this information from the CEO. He also wanted to make sure that his employees had the opportunity of a soft landing during this transition.

I was at first shocked and then amazed that everyone in the bank had been given this information. I was incredibly touched that the CEO would trust all of us with this very vital information. No one in the bank broke the code of confidentiality, although the bank was not successful and eventually merged with another large regional bank. However, the jobs and careers of hundreds of employees were saved because of the integrity of my CEO, who shared information with everyone in the bank. This experience is my benchmark for integrity and for caring for employees and an organization.

Focus on Strengths

"We confide in our strength, without boasting of it; we respect that of others, without fearing it."
Thomas Jefferson

At the time, I did not understand the concept of the power of synergy. However, I soon found out that it means one plus one is sometimes greater than two.

My best boss paired me up on a project with another employee who I was not particularly fond of working with. We were both trainers and the woman who was assigned to be my partner was very skilled at creating workbooks and doing research. My strengths were in the front of the room—it was easy for me to make people laugh and it always seemed that being in front of the room was effortless. Typically, I was surprised they actually paid me to do this job. However, I was always missing the deadline for creating workbooks. I could sense my manager was becoming a little frustrated with this shortcoming.

When my boss assigned the project of working together, I questioned her ability to lead. I wondered how my boss could put us together; we do not even like each other, much less working together. Nevertheless, she said our strengths matched—whatever that meant.

Therefore, we worked on a few projects. She would create the workbooks and do the research

43

and I would read the workbooks and use my front room skills to educate and entertain. After awhile it became apparent we were jelling as a team, but we still were not particularly fond of each other.

However, after a year I began to realize what my boss meant by the power of synergy. The two of us together were able to produce more and better training programs. We were able to produce more than we could ever produce by ourselves. My best boss ever, knew the power of synergy, by putting teams together and looking at each of our individual strengths and weaknesses, she was able to create a stronger team. She recognized that I was strong in front of the room and she knew that my new partner was very strong in research and developing workbooks. The employees got a much better training program and they got our great workbook that they could use as a reference tool long after the training session had ended, which helped to reinforce their learning. In addition, they got my storytelling and my humor, which allowed the ideas to stick. At first, I thought this arrangement was absurd, but after working with it for over a year and a half, I began to realize the power of synergy. I had to tip my hat to my best boss, because she had used that power of synergy to create a very strong training team.

My recommendation to all managers is to use the power of synergy to create a stronger team. The other great lesson is that my boss did not try to fix our weaknesses. She recognized our weaknesses—she overlooked them—but she utilized our strengths. A year later, I asked her how she came up with the idea. She said she had read the book "First Break All the Rules" by Marcus Buckingham and she recognized the power of focusing on peoples' strengths. She said when she was a new manager, she tried to focus on fixing weaknesses, but she realized this is a futile attempt at absurdity. She said, "You cannot take an introvert, send them to Dale Carnegie training for two weeks and turn them into Martin Luther King." She said, further, that you could take an extrovert, send them to Dale Carnegie training and make them a much better speaker. She said now she just tries to focus on utilizing peoples' strengths and minimizing their weaknesses, or balancing their weaknesses through team member strengths. She said by putting us together she took my strengths of presentation skills and my partner's strength of research and documentation and made us a much better team. The two things I walked away with from this learning point was to use the power of synergy and focus on peoples' strengths. If I can do that as a manager in the future, I can make an impact on the lives of the employees I work with and I can make a strong impact on the organization I work at. If I can do those two things then it was worth it for me to have chosen the path of being a manager.

Leave a Legacy
Arnold Sandbothe

"No legacy is so rich as honesty."
William Shakespeare

I have worked for some of the best-known managers in some of the largest organizations represented in my trade association. However, none of them stand out as my best boss ever.

In fact, my best boss ever was a manager from central Missouri who was in charge of a small financial institution. Rarely did she have more than six or seven people on her staff at one time. However, her talent was not in the number of people she led, but in her ability to turn her staff, no matter how small, into leaders and managers.

She would instill in them the belief that they could take over a key and significant role in an organization. She was able to guide six employees to become CEOs of other financial institutions. That is why she was the best manager I ever saw. She left a legacy and helped six other people achieve accomplishments that they may never have achieved without her help.

My wish for all managers is that at their retirement party, people will come up and say, "Because of your belief in me with your coaching, mentoring and support, I was able to achieve..." Of course, you can build buildings and build a lot of wealth, but on your deathbed, the question you will ask yourself if you helped build people. Did I leave my organization and community better than I found it?

That is the essence of a real manager—a true leader. It is someone who helped be the difference in the lives of others. If you can do that, you can leave this world knowing you made a difference.

Compliment

"I can live for two months on a good compliment."
                                        Mark Twain

My favorite boss knew the power of a compliment. One day he was walking by my office. He zoomed passed the door because he was always in a hurry, stopped abruptly, turned around and popped into my office. He said "Good Morning, Julie! You did a great job on the newsletter article concerning IRA's. That was great stuff on the power of compound interest and how compound interest grows over time. Keep up the excellent work; our clients need that kind of information. Compound interest is one of the most powerful tools our clients have and you did a great job showing them that power over a lifetime. Thanks for the article."

Then he smiled and was gone. Poof! It was like a drive-by compliment. He just stops, gives you a compliment and then he is gone.

When I was promoted to management, I went to him and asked him how he gives such effective compliments. He said, "I use the power of five S's." I asked what they were and he asked me to sit, take out a yellow pad and write down the recipe.

Five S's Recipe:
- Short
- Sweet
- Soon
- Sincere
- Specific

He went on further to say, "The compliments need to be short, not too long. They need to be nice—that is the sweet part. They need to be soon, because compliments go bad with age. They need to be specific. I will fire a manager who just writes on the annual evaluation form 'good job.' The compliment and reinforcement needs to be specific: reward the behavior you want and continue to recognize it. The more specific the compliment or reinforcement, the more power the compliment has. That leads to specific; if the compliment is specific then it will be more sincere."

Since I had seen him use this technique hundreds of times, I had many examples of its effectiveness. By using the power of the five S's that made him one of the best bosses, I had ever worked for in my entire life.

Be an Arbiter

My best boss was also the toughest. He would not let disagreements in the office grow to the point of explosiveness. As a teller in a financial institution, my best boss would settle disagreements or teach us how to settle those disagreements.

There was another teller in the office and we did not really get along too well. Sometimes personalities are just different. The relationship between the two of us continued to deteriorate and the signs of tension were visible to everyone. Once it got the point where we were barely talking, the boss summoned us into his office. This was as pleasant as a root canal without anesthesia.

He invited both of us to sit down in the conference room and to share what was going on. He wanted us to get the problem out on the table. However, he set some ground rules for how discussion would go. First off, one of us would share their side of the story and then the other would share their side of the story. Finally, we would work out the differences between the two of us. However, once the other person talked I could not state my position without restating her position in my own words to her satisfaction. And, vice a versa; she could not respond to my position without first restating what I said in her own words to my satisfaction. This was the hardest thing to ever learn at work.

It is not human nature to restate the other person position in your own words to their satisfaction before you respond. Normally, in an argument you just restate or scream your point of view repeatedly. This forced you to listen to their point of view and to restate it before you were able to respond.

She said the problem stemmed from a time when I was in a hurry and I seemed to throw paperwork at her station rather than to hand it to her and ask politely. From that moment on, things just continued to escalate. She said, "I did not think you liked me and so everything you did just grew out of proportion." I told her I meant no harm and could not even remember the time it occurred. That is classic about disagreements, they just continue to grow. By sitting us down and using this technique, it helped me in the rest of my work world because I learned to listen first, and paraphrase before I responded. That was an incredibly helpful tool in my life. It was one of the hardest skills to learn, especially if you are angry with someone, but it helped get everything out in the open and we were able to work together because we learned to talk that way with each other when the situation got tense.

Teacher and Mentor
Jeff Varney

"Experience is the worst teacher. It always gives the test first and the instruction afterward."

Zig Ziglar

The late Lynn Gernert was the best boss I have ever had.

In the formative years of my professional growth, Lynn Gernert, earned my respect and admiration with everything he did.

As a recent college graduate working as an engineer in my very first job, I was surrounded by colleagues of my age and education level who were doing the grunt work. For them it was a very challenging time in their career, they did not sign on to do calculation after calculation. They wanted to be challenged and they wanted to do some higher-level thinking. However, they were not as lucky as I was because, Lynn Gernert was my manager.

Lynn did not assign me menial tasks of a repetitive nature. He would give me a vision of the task because he had the ability to sit down with that vision on a piece of paper and to convey that vision to me. With Lynn, I did not feel like I was an employee; I felt like I was a colleague and a partner in the project, even though this was my very first job right out of college. Once he assigned the task to me and he was always successful in his vision instruction. However, once I had the task assigned, he gave me the latitude and the leeway to do it my way. The task did not always have to be done his way. He understood that creative and educated people could come up with a variety of ways to solve a problem.

Lynn also recognized my abilities and could sense when I could only take on so much of a project. He would allow me to work as far as I could and then he would wait for me to come back for additional instruction.

The real skill was his ability to keep me in the industry when my other college friends were not challenged and wanted to go into another field of endeavor. They were given grunt work and repetitive processes and it drove them nuts. However, with Lynn's help, I was given the opportunity to do very interesting things.

The best thing about Lynn was his ability to always learn. That challenged me to always learn too. Those were his best skills to inspire me to think and work through projects, to continue to learn and grow and to give me interesting work. Now that I am a manager, I try to emulate his style.

Open to Feedback

"To be a teacher in the right sense is to be a learner. I am not a teacher, only a fellow student."
Soren Kierkegaard

When I was first hired, I was informed that I would be part of the team that would evaluate my boss. I was shocked and surprised that part of my role would be to give feedback to my boss.

However, this feedback was the basis for why she was one of my best bosses ever.

After I was on the job for about two months, my boss came to me and handed me an evaluation form. Here were some of the sample questions and we were to rank them on a scale of one to four. The reason they used this scale system was so no one could just pick three as the average. Your response had to either be above or below-average.

SAMPLE QUESTIONS:
- Admits mistakes?
- Communicates effectively in meetings?
- Manages conflicts to a productive outcome?
- Develops employees?
- Keeps confidences?
- Dresses appropriately?
- Does not take credit for others' work?
- Does not play favorites?

There were many more questions than just this, but the power of the process was that my manager would invite all the raters to a conference room and then have an open discussion about the feedback. Not everyone would go, but the ones who did attend gave some very constructive feedback and her strength as a manager was her ability to intently listen to what was being said. She worked at listening and taking the comments to heart.

There were some things said in those meetings that were painful and difficult for her to swallow, but they were said out of care and concern. You could tell she worked at taking the information to heart. By her openness and willingness to listen, it set a tone for the entire department. Everyone tried to be more open and to listen more carefully. You could tell after the meetings it made a difference with everyone.

The amazing thing was the impact it made on the entire company. As a manager, she grew and became better because of the feedback she was getting. However, the company did not endorse nor use 360-degree feedback. Nevertheless, once word got around that she was using it and the results were positive, within two years the Human Resources Department used her method and taught it to other managers.

This simple technique changed my first day of being hired, because I was invited to be part of the feedback team for my boss, but it also changed our department, and then ultimately changed our company, because the entire company started to use her method. By watching her work at improving herself, she helped improve the discussions in the entire company.

Ask Questions

"He who asks a question is a fool for five minutes; he who does not ask a question remains a fool forever."
Chinese Proverbs

My best boss ever was great at asking questions.

A client called us about making changes to their website. We were just about finished with the project, so I asked my manager if we could have a phone conference with the client. We were all on the phone and the client said, "The logo needs to be bigger." In my estimation, the logo was already large enough. I could have articulated several reasons why I did not think making it any bigger was the best direction for the site. However, before I could respond, my manager asked the client "Why do you want the logo bigger?" After some discussion, the client expressed his concern that the brand of the site was not prominent enough. They did not feel like, when you first hit the home page, you would immediately know and understand you were at www.whatever.com. Aha! Now we have a problem. See, "Make the logo bigger" is a solution. "The brand is not prominent enough" is a problem. The skill of my manager was that he could ask questions of the client and then let them tell him where they wanted to go with the project.

In an ideal world, it is the client's job to bring problems and the designers' job to find solutions. I did not end up making the logo bigger. I did put more white space around it and added a subtle (but effective) watermark of the brand icon in a very prominent position on the page. The point is this: making the logo bigger was only one possible solution to the problem.

Whenever I wanted to get into a discussion with a client or a co-worker and my boss was present, he would always listen and respond with questions. His goal was always to understand the other person better.

Supportive

I have the greatest boss in the world. I had only been with the company a few weeks, when my father passed away. My mother was devastated— he had a heart attack and he died suddenly. My youngest brother was only 13 years old and it was awful on him. Right at the age where you need a role model and he is gone. Josh cried like a baby at the funeral. The whole thing broke my heart. However, the day he died I went in to work and planned to continue to work everyday except the day of the funeral, because I needed the money to help cover the expenses for the funeral as well as normal living expenses. I had the job for only three weeks and had been unemployed for several months before that. A friend in the office knew that my family was going through a hard time and shared that information with my boss. My attitude was that you have to do what you have to do. My boss called me into his office and he handed me a check for two weeks pay and said, "Take as much time as you need because family is the most important thing." I cried like a baby all the way home. I will never forget what he did for me, because he gave me the opportunity to be there with my mother and my brother.

He is great in other ways too, but his sensitivity to the challenges that I faced at the time is still appreciated. You never forget people who really help you out when you face a crisis.

Everybody is Valuable

"Those whom we support hold us up in life."
Marie Ebner von Eschenbach

My boss actually had me believing that nothing in the world could keep us from being successful. To make matters even more interesting, he taught us how to give others that same feeling. He showed us how to be successful and how to lead others to success. Here is an example of that and how he put the lesson to action.

My boss walked in to my office and asked what was wrong. I did not tell him the entire story, but I told him that my son had a problem; he lost his driver's license for a year and lost his job because he could not drive back and forth to work. We only live about three blocks from the office so he called my son and asked him to come in to talk to him, without me knowing about it. He owned a repair shop the other direction from our home and it needed a repairperson to help in the shop. He asked my son if he would like to do that. My son jumped at the chance to get a job that required no driving. When I got home from work that night, my son showed me $20 my boss had "advanced" him. He was going to work at my boss's other company and that would pay back the $20 advance loan.

However, the best things my boss taught my son was how to be responsible and how to be responsive in a positive way to customers. My boss said, "Everyone who walks in the door whether a customer, a fellow employee, or a manager—is valuable and we need to make sure we serve everyone to the best of our ability."

I was not the only one my boss helped. He treated all of his employees like they were family.

My Best Boss Ever

Listen

*"Listening, not imitation,
may be the sincerest form of flattery."*
Dr. Joyce Brothers

My company was smart to hang onto him. My boss was an electrical engineer but he did not know much about the new system we were designing. We were working on data transfer interface system between two clients, who needed to share data from two different mainframes.

Anytime esoteric things like data error transfer in the system would come up, he would take the time, maybe days, talking to the group to understand the real issue. There were times when he would agree with me and there were times when he would not. However, he always had the facts and heard all sides of the story before he made a decision on how we would handle it. You cannot resent someone like that. His ability to get all sides of an important issue was one of his strengths. He listened, digested and really understood before we made a major decision on how to put the project together. He was a master at getting input from everyone. No one ever resented his decisions because everyone knew it was a team process.

Contrast that to organizations where a few top people make a ton of money and all the managers are scrambling, politicking, and backstabbing for that next promotion. All the bosses are so busy kissing the behinds of the person above, they never have time to deal with or worry about their subordinates. It is exactly backwards of the way things should be. A good boss is concerned with getting his people up to speed and then he looks good because those people do well. This is very different from some of the people who fake it as bosses in many companies today.

I used to be a grumbler and thought that all bosses were a waste of money and time. This changed after listening to a friend talk about college basketball coaches. He pointed out that a coach could leave a winning team and go to a school full of kids that have been losing. A year later the coach's old team is losing and his new team with the same kids that were losers a year before are now winners. No, a boss can make a real difference and if you have a good one you are lucky indeed. We were lucky to have a boss that listened and helped us make decisions as a group.

The Power of Influence

In December of 2005, I had a job offer from another part of the company I was working for and I decided I was going to make the move. My current "boss" had the leadership skills of a kindergartner on a tirade. Everything was done for him because, "I told you to do it." Having the offer to move away from this tyrant, I was quick to take up the offer.

However, the organization loved me and wanted me to stay. There was no way I was going to continue to work for that man, though. My upper management came in to my office one day. All they did was say this other boss's name. They looked me square in the eye and said, "We'll make Bob your boss." I looked back, my eyes raised and responded, "I'll stay." I let them woo me a little bit, of course, but as soon as I knew this man would become my boss, I was going to stay.

I had never worked for him before, but everyone who ever had him talked about how amazing he was. I had only heard of him by reputation but what a reputation he had! That is what you need—you need leadership. You need to manage and lead in such a way that people talk about you in a very positive light. In addition, my new boss, my best boss ever, was an amazing leader. His leadership reputation kept me working there; his skills retained me.

Discover the One Word
Dr. M. Dwane, MD

"One word
frees us of all the weight and pain of life:
That word is love."

Sophocles

My best boss ever was my residence director when I was a resident in Pennsylvania. His name was Nikitas Zervanos. I called him Dr. Z. He had incredible vision. Not only for the residence program, but his vision for each of us as individuals, and for our lives. I remember in my initial interview his incredible listening skills, and the questions he asked. He would typically interview between 100 and 120 people for the residency program, and only accept a few positions. Interestingly enough, when I interviewed with him, he wanted to know more than just about me and my work and what I would do for the program. He was interested in me as an individual and a family member. He asked about my family and what brought me to this point in my life. However, he said it in a way that showed he was truly interested in me; he was not fishing for information.

However, when I talk about his vision, he had the incredible ability to see the true character of a person. During the interview, he asked me to think of one word that best described me. Dr. Z said, "Before you tell me, I'm going to write down the one word that I think describes you." I

65

thought for a while, worried that it was going to be a trick question, and I said, I think if people had to describe me, they would say I was 'passionate.' He turned the paper around and it was written down the exact same word "passionate." I could not believe it, and I asked, "How in the world did you guess that?" He said that he could just tell, after hearing me talk, that I was passionate about my work, my family, and my life. He recognized that I invested a tremendous amount of emotional energy into everything that I did, and he said that was what would make me an incredible resident, because I had that passion. This was in the course of maybe 30 minutes. I was so impressed at how clear sighted he was. Other people said that he had done the same thing in their interview and that he was incredibly accurate in their interviews as well. He was able to describe everyone with great accuracy. When I work with people, I try to listen so deeply that I can pick that one word that describes them. I may not ask for it, but I try to listen as deeply as Dr. Z.

His patients adored him, but it was because he cared about them. He was a very direct person, but at the same time, he does it in such a way that you do not feel threatened or offended. You just feel enveloped in his caring attitude. My goal is to match Dr. Z's care for others.

Be On Their Boards of Directors

My best boss ever put all of his managers in a conference room and asked the following questions:

- Who were the people in your life that helped you to develop to who you are?
- Who has influenced you to become the person you are today?
- Who were the people that you would consider the Board of Directors of your life?

He then passed out a sheet of paper that looked like a boardroom diagram. On each chair, we were supposed to write down the names of people that we thought of, those people who were on our board of directors, those people who helped us to develop to this point.

After pondering the questions, we went around the room and shared stories of those very influential people who helped develop us and why.

People told stories about teachers, grandparents, little league coaches, and even class clowns. To each one, there was a very real reason why each person was on his or her board of directors.

My boss then asked, "Each of you manage a number of people. How many boardrooms are you on?" He challenged us to not be a manager, but a manager of influence. Then he said something that I will never forget.

"What is influence if you don't use it?"

I have never forgotten the boardroom exercise or the challenge he gave us that day. The people who made a difference in my life took an interest in me, and helped me see potential I did not think I had. It has made me a better manager and a better person. Lead so you leave a legacy and so that you make a difference in the lives of others. Manage so that you make the board of directors of your employees.

Considerate versus Inconsiderate
Joe Edwards

*"If people would be kind, considerate
and use common sense, Life would be easier."*
Peter Bonk

I have worked for both 50 percent and 150 percent bosses. While a 50 percent boss will take credit for your work, a 150 percent boss will turn that recognition around and beam it back to you. That is what a best boss does.

I was involved with a project in which I had contributed about 90 percent of the work. At the meeting where the proposal was pitched to the board, I sat quietly in the back of the room and waiting for my accolades. At the end of the meeting, the directors started to shake hands with my boss and offer their congratulations on such a great job. I sat in horror as he took the credit for the project from everyone. He even had the audacity to explain how much time the project had taken away from his family time. By the time I was able to escape the meeting, I was furious!

I continued to do my job, but I never went out of my way to cover his tail again. If he cannot provide me with 50 percent of the credit, why should I step out to take a bullet for him? Later that year, I was transferred to a new department. My former boss, having made enemies of his employees, did not have anyone to complete his

69

projects for him anymore, and was fired. Of course, I thought to myself, "karma."

With my new boss, Andrew, I soon learned the meaning for a 150 percent boss.

I had an important meeting with an even more important client. This meeting was going to be a make or break moment. This meeting was going to make or break my sales quota for the year. Yes, pressure. However, a 150 percent boss does the following. My best boss drove six hours, one way, to be there with me in the presentation. He offered me valuable information during the meeting. I believe that I would not have sold the client that day without his help. He had some specific knowledge that helped answer important questions for the client. They were under some serious time constraints and had they not received that information at that moment, they probably would have selected another vendor.

However, the most amazing thing was that he gave me all the credit for getting the business. I heard through a friend that he was mentioning to people what a great job I did to seal the deal at the board meeting. The respect and admiration that he gained from me was so incredible that I immediately went to the board to make sure that they knew how instrumental he was in getting the business. I did not want to take all the credit.

My 150 percent boss takes a real interest in not just me, but my family as well. He always asks about my kids—by name—and always wants to know how everyone is doing. That is the difference. You will only give 50 percent to help a 50 percent boss, but you will take a bullet, walk through fire, or give 150 percent effort to protect a 150 percent boss.

Am I Being Developmental or Critical
Margaret Williams

"It is easier to be critical than correct."
Benjamin Disraeli

My best boss ever was a man by the name of Glen Armanie. He was the executive vice-president and I was the vice-president at the time. Glen did not like doing the annual evaluations, but that did not mean it did not have to be done. As any good executive would, he performed the annual reviews and the appropriate information would go in the personnel file. The reason that Glen was my best boss was not because he followed protocol. It was because he let me evaluate him.

At first, I was surprised by his request and a little uncomfortable. Would I be committing career suicide if I said something critical of him? However, he laid those fears to rest when he said that all he was looking for was real input about his performance. I remember thinking, how different this was, but he even provided me with a list of questions to better evaluate him. No other boss had asked me to evaluate him or her—it was always the other way around. The annual review was a one-way street, and once they were done giving me their opinion, we were done; or at least I thought. Glen was different and his difference made him my best boss ever.

There was another huge difference about Glen. His perspective on communication was something that I will never forget about him. In our meetings and discussions, he would often add in his caveat, "Am I being critical or am I being developmental?" This simple question was the key difference between Glen and every other boss I have ever had.

He had the understanding of how to strive to make conversations developmental and not just critical. That difference made all of our conversations easier because we both knew that we were trying to help, not just criticize. It took the edge off all of our conversations and at times, resulted in us joking with each other about whether we were being critical or developmental.

Over time, we would even joke with each other, "Is this being developmental or is this being critical?"

We still laugh.

Re-brand

I had been at the company for six years when my old boss retired and I came under the care of my new boss, Shirley Walker. The first time I met her, she pulled me into her office, closed the door and said, "Well, you've been here for six years and I don't know who you are or what you've done." I about dropped dead! I thought my six years of pulling in clients and making sales had gone unnoticed. My old boss always said I did a great job. I replied, "What do you mean you don't know who I am?"

She smiled, "We need to re-brand you." To this day, she loves to tell people that she plucked me out of the garbage and dusted me off. At that time, I believed that I was successful. She showed me otherwise, in a caring but authoritative way. She showed me the perception that others in the organization had of me. She took it upon herself for the next two years to reposition me to be the best possibly. She showed me my sales numbers compared with others and told me that I was better than that. She demonstrated over the next two years that I could be a top performer. Up to this point, average and below average sales numbers were okay. I found that working with Shirley that first two years was a rude awakening.

After mentally comparing my old boss with Shirley, I immediately recognized a huge difference between the two. My old boss would tell me everything was going fine, Shirley was going to reveal the 'painful' truth. In this case, the truth had thorns. Another lesson I learned is that bosses who tell you what you want to hear, never help you develop.

As we left our first sales call, I could tell she looked upset. We drove in silence for almost a mile before she asked me if anyone had ever taught me how to sell. I had been doing this for years; I had average to below average numbers, but not awful. She said, "Okay, let us review what happened in there and see what we can learn from it. From the interview we just had, when do you think the client was ready to buy?" I replied that they were ready to buy when I asked for the business. Shirley said, "They were sold 20 minutes before that."

Shirley understood the selling process better than anyone that I had worked with before. She went on to show me some of the buying signals that I had missed. Before I worked with Shirley, I thought questions from the client like, "how long will it take to deliver it" were just questions of clarification. She showed me that *is* a buying question. When the client asks questions like that, give them a closing question. For example, "Would the 15th be a good day for delivery?" Let them pick the delivery date and when they do, then pick up the contract. They may ask more questions, but you are ready to close. She showed things that illuminated the sales process the way I had never seen it before. She told me that my presentation was over kill, and "When you've got'em, close'em." It was the first time that I had somebody be that honest with me. The straightforward feedback was both refreshing and frightening. My old boss never went on a sales call with me, nor was he this honest about my performance. Shirley did both, and it made a world of difference in my career.

About a year later, her 'honest' feedback was not sitting well with me. My frustration level at her level of candor was wearing thin. Every week I was applying for every new job posted in the company just to get away from her. She caught wind of my desire to leave. Finally, she sat me down and said, "If you leave now, you'll take this anger with you and you'll never get past it. You'll never reach your greatest potential." It stunned me like a "u-turn on an interstate at 70 miles an hour." I sat there and thought about it. I really wanted to leave. But the little voice of reason deep down inside said, "She can mentor you past this, and help repair your career." As they say, I stayed and it was a career choice.

Now six years later under her care and leadership, I have become one of the top sellers in the company. Before I was in that forgotten middle of the 'Average Joe's.' In the past couple of years, I have been asked to serve on company-wide committees in the development of new products, and asked for my feedback on the long-term strategic plans of the company. Before Shirley, I was never in the top 10 sales people of the company, and we have hundreds of sales people nationwide. Her ability to re-brand me was frightening and enlightening. However, I learned how to be a top 10 producer, not an average seller. I learned how to move around the corporate environment, whereas before, I would just shoot off at the mouth. Now I was more tempered. My ideas are more carefully thought out, and I only give feedback that would be helpful, rather than just spew the first opinion that pops into my head.

My old boss was never close to ever becoming my best boss. He never gave me the honest and some times painful feedback I needed to hear. Shirley took the leap of faith. She risked my anger to help me grow. It is obvious today she cares deeply about my success, but when I was first getting the feedback, all I saw was the criticism and not the care and concern.

Recently, she was going to be gone for two months, and she asked me to fill in for her. After she got back, she told me that she was proud of me. She said, "When I was preparing to leave, I could not think of anyone else but you to run my department in my absence." That was one of the best compliments I ever received.

If she had not coached me and been brutally honest, I would not have stayed. I would have never become a top 10 performer. It is true; she dusted off my career and polished me up. For that, she is my best boss ever.

Learn from Everything

"You better believe there will be times in your life when you'll be feeling like a stumbling fool. So take it from me: you'll learn more from your mistakes than anything that you could ever learn in school."

Billy Joel

In the army, you work with lots of heavy equipment. We are constantly moving trucks, moving equipment, and repositioning big stuff.

We were preparing for an exercise and a visit from the general. When a general appears for the type of exercise we were going to do, it is a big deal. To make matters worse, we were rushing around and trying to get everything set up. The rush of activity led to undesired results.

We had a private assigned to move a huge truck with a trailer attached to the back. He backed up, missed the brake, and slammed the trailer into a tree completely bending the trailer into an "A" frame shape. The private was so startled that he hit the gas, put the truck in gear and ran the front end of the truck into another tree, and smashed the entire front end. It was like watching a comedy skit. Unfortunately for all of us, the general showed up just moments before the crash and witnessed the whole debacle.

Once the private hit the tree, the truck stalled, a huge cloud of dust settled, and silence engulfed the area. The general then walked toward the truck. Everyone thought, "Oh my, this kid is done." The general climbed up on the truck so he could look in the driver's window. He asked the private, "Are you alright son?" The poor private was stunned. Here he had just made a huge mistake and the first time he meets a general is when he is peering into his wrecked truck window.

The general then asked, "Young man can you tell me what happened?" The private explained his error. Without being judgmental or aggressive in anyway he continued, "Private, what did you learn?" He said, "I needed to slow down and be more careful."

The general then smiled and replied, "Son, that is a valuable lesson. Now, let's get this mess cleaned up." He then jumped off the truck and went on his way—with entourage in tow. I learned a valuable lesson about leadership that day. When tragedy strikes, ask what happened and what was learned. There is no glory in ripping a hole in the other person's soul. That accomplishes nothing. What the general taught me was that there is a valuable lesson in everything. Even mistakes.

Focused Listening

"Listening is a magnetic and strange thing, a creative force. When we really listen to people there is an alternating current, and this recharges us so that we never get tired of each other.
We are constantly being re-created."
Brenda Ueland

My boss is the best boss ever simply because of his ability to make you his primary focus. Whenever you would walk in to talk to him, no matter how minuscule, he would take his focus completely away from whatever he was doing and focus only on you. His BlackBerry would be put away on silent, and his desk would be cleared. When talking to my best boss, I felt that I was the only person that mattered. Being made to feel important made all the difference in the world. I mattered, and to tell you the truth that is all that mattered.

Trust in Me
Russ Jenisch

I was the scoreboard operator for the Cincinnati Reds, a job I just recently left to become a media consultant. I had worked for the Reds for the last 19 years, but my best boss ever was John Allen, the former COO of the Reds. He gave me the marching orders, "Do whatever you want with the scoreboard operation, you do your job and I will stay out of your way. Just don't embarrass me or the organization." He hired good people and he let them do their jobs. For all of that I admired him. He did not micromanage and he let me operate the scoreboard.

With the philosophy never to embarrass the Reds or John, I would make sure I did not do anything stupid. For example, one of my scoreboard colleagues developed the "Mullet Cam." This is where between innings they would zoom in with the ballpark cameras and show guys on the scoreboard that looked like Billy Ray Cyrus on a bad day. He got in trouble with that one. Certainly, it was funny, but keeping to the philosophy of doing my job and not embarrassing the Reds or John was the key to my long-term success.

- Hire good people, trust your people, and get out of their way.
- My best boss gives me the expectations and tells me to have at it.

■ He told me not to embarrass him or the organization.

One day within the first two years of Great American Ball Park, a fire system tripped and the strobe light was going off. The pitcher was in his wind up, but stopped as soon as the alarm went off. We did not make any public announcements because it had been going off all week when the Reds were not playing. We made a public announcement that said there is no fire and to not be alarmed. Then about an inning or two later, I decided to show a film of rolling fire on the scoreboard like a fireplace and then I played the song, "Burning Down the House" by the Talking Heads. I thought it was funny, but someone called to complain. He said his daughter could not sleep because she was afraid of the fire images "burned into her head." I did not mean to offend anyone and fortunately, it did not rank as one of the most embarrassing moments for the Reds. However, it was a mistake.

As an employee, we always have to be aware of what the ramifications are and to be careful with the image of the organization. I respected John so much I never wanted to harm his reputation or the reputation of the Reds.

Recognized Talent

"I have no particular talent. I am merely inquisitive."
Albert Einstein

I had recently changed jobs. My new boss appeared to be a standoffish and a rather mean person. As part of the training process, I had to complete an eight person five-day training class. Afterward, I was called into my boss's office. I thought I had done something terribly wrong. Instead, she explained that she saw potential in me that even I had not seen yet! She concluded our meeting by telling me that she knew I would be a leader in that company someday. She said she saw 'David in the marble.' I asked, "What does that mean?"

She said "It is the story of Michelangelo and his search for a piece of marble big enough to be his masterpiece." Then she told me this story.

> Sometimes serious limitations lead an artist to produce his greatest work. Look at the David, which came from a ruined block no one else wanted.

> Michelangelo had heard about a big block of marble 18 feet high that was sitting around in a yard. He went to the town hall to ask about it and was told that the mayor had promised it to a sculptor called Sansovino. Another official said he had heard it was meant for Leonardo da Vinci.

83

In any case, the best thing would be for Michelangelo to forget about it because it was worthless.

"Didn't they tell you?" said the official. "A fellow called Simone da Fiesole started to carve a statue years ago and the fool began by drilling a big hole right through the block. If it had been a clean hole maybe something could still be done; but then he goes and chips half the stone away from front and back of the hole too. A dozen sculptors have gone to look at it and they all come back here either angry or nearly crying. It was a beautiful block too, without any flaws. Da Fiesole ought to be hanged."

Michelangelo knew the story and he had often wondered just how bad the botch was and whether he could not cut a figure out of that block, hole and all. That a dozen other sculptors had not been able to do that did not mean a thing to him. "Can I at least go and see it?" he asked.

In the yard of the Office of Works, Michelangelo spent a long time at the stone. He walked around it, took measurements, stood in front of it in thought.

"Now you see for yourself why everyone else rejected the darn thing," said the old caretaker with all the keys. However, he got no answer from Michelangelo.

As soon as he was home, Michelangelo started drawing and making a little wax model of a David, which had been da Fiesole's subject. When he was sure he could carve his figure out of the botched block, he asked the mayor, Soderini, to give it to him.

He carved the David, according to Condivi, though few believe this, in 18 months and "extracted the statue so exactly that the old rough surface of the marble [and da Fiesole's chisel marks] still appear on the top of the head and on the base."

After she told me that story, she said she saw the potential in me. Even though I was not a discarded piece of marble, she still saw my potential. That simple conversation made me look at myself in a completely new light. Since others saw potential in me, I began to see the potential myself. She was right; I stayed many years and did become a leader in the company. I honestly never would have acted with that mindset had she not seen "David in the marble."

Promote

"My best boss was more interested in promoting me than promoting himself."

Teambuilding

When I was a kid, actually a teenager, I worked at a movie theater doing the simple tasks, selling tickets, selling popcorn or cleaning the theater. We were always busy on the weekends, but during the week, when it was slower, our boss would take a group of us water skiing.

It was a great team-building event and I got good at water skiing. We even went skiing in February near Denver Colorado. As you can imagine it was cold! It was so cold at times, he even had to take the boat out and break up the ice. We got so good at water skiing that we could jump off the dock so we did not have to get wet; of course, he provided wetsuits for everyone. It was always great fun, and it kept everyone motivated. I did not want to screw up at work and risk not being invited back again. That happened to some employees. Bad choices can lead to negative consequences.

The key to the whole thing was that it was a great team-building event. It brought all of us together in a non-work, fun environment. It was fun and it helped us build friendships.

It helped when we needed to get something done fast, we knew how to work together as a team.

Wander Around

"Management By Interacting and Walking Around."
Mark Hamister

My best boss ever came from Hewlett Packard before he worked for the financial institution we were at together. As a teller, I only saw my bosses when my teller drawer was out of balance or someone complained about my service. Other than that, I never saw them. They managed by staying in their office. However, my best boss would come out and talk to us.

The first time he came out of his office, he asked "What can I do to make your jobs easier or better?" I was shocked; no boss had ever done that before. Three of us shared a phone in the teller area, and we would trade off on who's turn it was to answer the phone. Since we only had one corded phone for three people it was a nightmare. So I piped up, "Why not get a phone?" He asked, "Why do you need another phone?" We told him about the challenge of sharing the phone. He said no problem, and bought each of us our own phone. That may not seem like a big deal, but it was the first time that a manager had ever really paid attention to me as an employee in a non-negative way. It was refreshing to say the least.

A few months later, I was leaving the company because of a promotion with another company. I had any exit interview with this boss. He had an object on his desk that looked like an abacus. I asked what it was for. He said at Hewlett Packard you had to move those 30 beads every month. I inquired, "How do you move them?" He replied, "You move one every time you go wandering around." He went on to say, "At HP they were out for everyone to see, so your employees and other managers could see the beads moving. There were 10 red beads, 10 yellow beads and 10 green beads, and you always wanted to be in the green zone by the end of the month. If you did not move enough beads, everyone knew it. That is how I first learned about your challenge with the phone. I was moving a bead and wandering around the office."

After I left and became a manager at my new company, I got an abacus that I could use as a manager. It was my bead counter to remind me to wander around. My best boss made me a better boss and gave me something that I will never forget. The bead counter still sits on my desk.

Negatives Up and Positives Down

*"Few things in the world
are more powerful than a positive push. A smile.
A word of optimism and hope. And you can do it when
things are tough."*
Richard M. DeVos

He was the most positive person I ever knew. Nothing would ever bring him down, and he never brought anyone else down either.

After I was promoted to a management position within the company, he shared one of his management secrets with me. He leaned over at a conference one time, after hearing me complain about something in front of some of my employees. He almost whispered it, like he did not want anyone else to hear. He just said, "Negatives up, and positives down." I said "What?" He responded, "Never pass a negative comment or idea down to your employees."

After thinking about it for a while, I realized, I had never heard him say anything negative in front of his employees, ever. Certainly, I was a little embarrassed that day, but I took his idea to heart, and I never did it again.

Calm Under Crisis

"Be like a duck. Calm on the surface, but always paddling like the dickens underneath."
Michael Caine

IT managers tend to be wound just a little tight. If everything is going great, their fear is that the next great disaster is just around the corner. When disaster does strike, get out of the way. Therefore, they live on that fabled edge. They just avoided a crisis or they are in one. There is no calm in their minds, before or after the storm.

Steve Holahan was different though. Crises happen but they do not define him like they did for other IT managers. Early on in his career at Dupont, a crisis struck. All the phone lines lit up like a Christmas tree. I did not know what the problem was, but the person on the other end of the line would clue me in on what happened. It seems that one of the employees was deleting some files from the server and accidentally deleted some active files. Their deletion brought down computers for many people all over the plant.

That is when the typical IT manager goes nuts, and tries to find the culprit to ration out the appropriate punishment. Not Steve. It was fortunate for that technician who discovered his own mistake and fixed it relatively quickly. When Steve walked in their work area the problem was fixed and the phones had died down. Rather than

91

walking in and saying, "What the $#&@ just happened," he walks in and says, "Thanks for fixing the problem so quickly!" He then proceeded to ask what happened. He listened carefully and he was not judgmental.

He then asked if there were a way to make sure we have procedures so this does not happen again. The crew brainstormed some methods and then decided on a procedure. Since then, it has worked flawlessly. However, the respect that Steve has earned has been tremendous. He is a calm influence in the turbulent waters of IT. Employees know they can approach him with a challenge and he will listen.

With our past manager, if anything went wrong we would go nuts worrying about the repercussions, but not with Steve, we do not have to worry about all the nonsense; we can just do our job. As a team, we no longer have to worry about managerial blowups. He really does allow us to sail in calmer waters.

Invest in Growth

"Do you want my one-word secret of happiness? It's growth - mental, financial, you name it."
Harold S. Geneen

My best boss ever was my first CEO. Being new to the company, I had many unique ideas that most managers would have brushed away. However, instead of telling me that my ideas "weren't how things were done here," he gave me room to implement my thoughts. He had the trust in me to allow me to create an entirely new position in the company. I was allowed to write up the new job description and even create the pay scale for it. I got the job and the pay raise, because of his trust and support.

His best skill was being a mentor. A mentor believes in your ideas and helps you get them implemented. He had the time to walk me through the steps to present my ideas to the leadership team so the new job could be created. His trust made me realize that what I thought mattered to, not only him, but to the company as well. That feeling of importance was the key. He had a way of making me believe that my ideas had merit and they were worth pursuing. His trust and belief were the keys of getting me to where I am today.

Watch and Wait

"Watch your thoughts, for they become actions.
Watch your actions, for they become character.
Watch your character, for it becomes your destiny."

A friend from our local Chamber of Commerce came by one afternoon to discuss a job opening she had available at her corporation. She explained all the details, the pay, and the needed qualifications for employment. She then asked if I knew of anyone who would be interested in the job. As she was explaining the job qualifications, I realized that it was the perfect job for me!

In reality, she had watched me for some time in the Chamber, and realized I was always willing to volunteer for tasks and committees. She already had me in mind as a potential employee but waited for the right job to open up for me. Her reason for the visit was simply to see if I was interested in the position. She clearly knew what she was looking for even before she needed it.

Now, as a manager, I use her technique of always being on the look out for good talent. A simple question may be the first step to a job interview.

Increase Visibility
Pat Holley

"We have always understood that visibility is viability."
Marie Wilson

Kathleen Murphy is the president of a large trade association in Maryland and she is my best boss ever.

As president, she could make all the presentations to the board of directors on behalf of staff, and that would be fine. However, Kathleen wanted to increase senior staff's visibility within the organization. As she says, "everyone needs to shine," so she set it up so that I would make professional and business development reports to the board of directors. The visibility this allows me is important. It gives me the opportunity to establish relationships and rapport with our key leadership but it also allows me to highlight my team's work to the board. To let them know the progress we have made, and not only show the organization's accomplishments but personal contribution as well. This simple illustration really shows how she runs the entire organization, her care and concern for her employees is always evident. She makes all of us feel important and that we matter. With some managers it is all about them, with her, it is about all of us. She makes us all feel like family and that we are all key contributors to our success.

95

If I have one piece of advice for managers, it is that they give their employees an opportunity to shine. Kathleen continues to give me that opportunity and for that I am grateful.

Supporter

"The beginning of knowledge is the discovery of something we do not understand."

Frank Herbert

I had just moved from a small bank to a much larger one. In my previous job, I was allowed to voice my worries, concerns, and ideas without fear of rejection. At my old job, I was a big fish in a small pond, now I was in strange water. I was now a little bitty fish in a gigantic pond. I did not know the culture, the challenges, or the way to present ideas. My old ways were no longer effective. I was swimming in shallow water to protect myself.

If I offered ideas for implementation at the new bank, they were ignored; I just did not have the same influence as I had at my old bank. The fear that I had lost my influence set in, and that fear began to destroy my confidence. I thought about leaving and going back to safer waters.

However, my best boss ever, intervened. She sat me down and said, "If you go back now, you may never stretch and grow again. This is an opportunity to grow and you can do it." Then she taught me how to temper my opinions so that they could be presented in a more effective way. She taught me how to ask other employees opinions to build supportive coalitions before the idea was formally presented to the leadership team. She taught me how to make budget proposals, and

97

PowerPoint presentations that would answer the important questions before they came up. With her help, I was able to voice my opinion, but also protect my reputation in my job. Without her help, I would have left the company, and not have had the opportunity of growth that this challenge presented. Now I am a bigger fish, still in the gigantic pond. Who knows, one day I may be a big fish here?

Vacation Time

Aaron Otten
Regional Manager, Joe's Crab Shack

"Laughter is an instant vacation."
Milton Berle

My best boss ever is my current boss. I have worked for him about 18 months and he has many outstanding skills, but his best skill is his care and concern for his managers. Working for Joe's Crab Shack and traveling the country as we regional managers do, is a very demanding and challenging responsibility. There is always something to be done, and at times, it appears like you can never get away.

That is where vacation time comes in. The company gives us great vacation benefits, so we do not go insane! Some regional managers will take vacation time but still check emails, call their shops, and check in periodically. From their communications, it does not seem like they are really taking a vacation at all. My boss directs many hard-charging and focused people. They are all smart, talented, and ambitious. Having those traits got them the jobs they currently hold. One day while talking with my best boss he lamented, "We have managers who're taking vacation, but they really aren't on vacation." He asked, "Do you have any suggestions about it?" At that very moment, I did not, but I was flattered he would ask my opinion and seek out my advice. To

99

be honest, I was probably even guilty of the crime a couple of times.

A week later, we were talking on the phone and he said, "I've noticed that managers really aren't using their vacation time. Because of that, I have made a decision. I am going to fine managers who used their BlackBerry or checked emails while they were on vacation. I will just deduct it from their bonus checks." He said, "Family time is too important to not focus on your family. When you are at work, work, and when you are home, be home. When you are all on vacation, be on vacation."

I remember thinking, "Wow, a boss who actually cares about his employees. He knows if we are not recharged and refreshed from time to time, we cannot do the best job possible." My respect and admiration grew even more that day because he had the employees' best interests at heart. He cared about our family life, not just the job.

Work in the Trenches
Renee Johnson

I worked in the northeast United States. My best boss, Anthony Jennings was the Executive Vice-President at the time. Being in the northeast in the winter, there was a terrible blizzard. I lived probably 15 minutes from the office and it took me an hour to get there. It probably would have been faster to walk!

I remember that with the storm, few people made it into the office that day. By the time I got there, Anthony already had the lights on and the coffee warmed. At lunchtime, he ordered food so we all would not have to leave the office.

The thing I remember most though, was his ability to take up the fight. Since no one was in the office, there was no one there to take the mail around to everyone. Realizing this, Anthony took off his blue blazer and donned the mail jacket. He walked around and distributed the mail that day.

It demonstrated that someone of that caliber was willing to do what it takes to get things done. Someone to roll up his sleeves and work in the trenches. It set the example for me that nothing was too small or meaningless to do. You need to be able to manage strategy, but if you need to roll up your sleeves and pack boxes, you pack boxes.

Trustworthy
Bob Hoyle

"The only way to make a man trustworthy is to trust him."
Henry Stimson

My best boss ever had a highly ethical standard. He showed me how that was good business. We were to run a clean operation in terms of the bidding process.

We had private label products and various manufacturers would bid on those products to manufacture them. He asked us to always honor the bidding process. We constantly had people who would come in and say, "Here's the bid that you had, but I can undercut that by 5%." However, with the standards he set, you would have to say, "I can't do that." He knew that you could make money in the short-term that way, but in the long term, you would not.

He caught someone making a bid to one of our buyers saying that he would cut the price by 8% on our lowest bid. My boss physically threw the man out of the office and screamed at him, "We follow the rules, a bid is a bid. Never run your shadow over my door again." Shocked, I summoned the courage to go into his office later that day and asked, "Why'd you do that?"

His reply was simple, but something that I will never forget. "When everyone knows that the bidding process is honest, you'll have more bidders. If we have more bidders, overall we will get better prices. And more manufacturers wanting our business." That is how he led.

He said, "Everyone needs to understand the customer, everyone needs to understand what they go through on a day to day basis." He would hold a meeting, say that he wanted everyone to spend a week in the field, even accounting and finance people. He made sure that everyone talked to customers. He was the first one to sign up to spend the week on the road with customers.

That is why we were the most profitable drug chain in America on a per square-foot basis, and a return on investment basis. The man did not command, he set the example.

Coach for Your Position

"Good coaches teach respect for the opposition, love of competition, the value of trying your best, and how to win and lose graciously."

Brooks Clark

I was at a savings and loan for about three months and I was only 21. My boss, Bill, called me into his office and asked me what I wanted to do in the company. We had about thirty minutes of small talk before he finally coaxed the truth out of me.

I admitted I wanted his job.

He smiled at the response and replied, "Alright, let's go get it." In the next year and a half, he molded me into a perfect candidate for his position.

When he received a promotion, I took over his old job! It was Bill's ability to see my potential, give me the freedom to choose it, and enabled me to achieve it that made him my best boss ever.

Be There
Duncan McCallum

"Reflect on your present blessings, of which every man has many; not on your past misfortunes, of which all men have some."
Charles Dickens

He was the warden of the maximum-security prison in Huntsville, Texas. He was my best boss ever because he was consistent. He knew the rules and what it took to run a prison. It takes a lot more than just bars and guards. The truth is that guards and offenders are doing time together. You are both under strict conditions, you have to eat at a certain time, and you cannot do certain things.

As a prison guard, you are outnumbered 50:1. If the prisoners decide at some point that they are not going to do something, they are not. The warden was a great motivator in that he could motivate us to work with some horrific people. He never said, "Do it because I said so." That would have been easy. He helped us to see the bigger picture and to be part of the team.

Did we make mistakes? Sure, we did, but he always said, "A mistake of the mind, I can forgive, but a mistake of the heart is unforgivable." A mistake of character is completely different than just a brain burp. He would pull your best qualities to the surface and act on those, or pull out your worst ones and shine a light on them.

105

You would know very quickly if this were a business for you. He did not mess around in his leadership style, he did not have time for it, and we were there to run a prison. He needed to know right away if you were the right kind of person to do it.

I felt like I could always talk to him. He was very approachable and extremely respectable. If we lost something, he would come out into the field with us and try to find it. It would probably be 105 degrees outside, and he would be right out there with you.

Shortly after I started to work at the prison, I was hit by a tractor while riding my motorcycle. The first person to come to see me was my warden. For a maximum-security prison warden to leave his post and come do something like that was unheard of. I did not do anything special to deserve the treatment.

Powerful Lessons

"Remember, there are no mistakes, only lessons. Love yourself, trust your choices, and everything is possible."
Cherie Carter-Scott

I worked with my best boss through several years and a few different organizations. In all those years, he taught me two powerful lessons. Care for the employee's welfare, and care for the employee's temptations.

One day we were discussing an insurance premium increase. It was only a $2 per pay period increase. It did not really seem like a lot of money at all, but he was worried that it would be too much of a hardship on the employees. It showed how dedicated to the employees he was. It proved to me that managers have a responsibility to the people—beyond just the company.

The second powerful idea came one day during training. He told me, "If you put temptation in someone's way and they succumb, you are partly at fault." It showed me that you had to have those preventative measures out there to protect not just the company, but the employees as well. Now I always make sure that systems are in place to protect the company and protect the employee.

Support When Most Needed
Kati Lazzari

"As long as you derive inner help and comfort from anything, keep it."
Mahatma Gandhi

My grandmother raised me since I was three years old. Both of my parents were deceased, so I relied heavily on her my entire life. In every sense, she was my mother. She raised me in California, but I moved to Virginia, while my husband was on active duty for the military.

She had been ill for several months and I soon received word from her doctor that it was time for me to come home to see her before she passed away. I approached my supervisors and requested time off to go see her. To my surprise, they told me that if I left now, I would not be able to go home to attend her funeral. They said, keep my job and do it their way, or lose my job and get a chance to see my grandmother for the last time. Although I hated their decision, it was an easy choice for me. I would leave to go see my grandmother and stay until she passed. Then I would inform them that I no longer worked for them. I only have one family, but there are many jobs.

A few years later, I moved with my husband to New Orleans. I soon began working at NAS JRB Credit Union. Shortly after we arrived, my father-in-law became terminally ill. He had a lung transplant that was now being rejected. During this troubling time, I spend the first few months just trying to get everything in order for my mother-in-law and father-in-law. My husband was on active duty and deployed overseas, so I had to get the paperwork in for him to come home. The credit union I was working for and my best bosses—Helen Delin and Andre Theall—genuinely cared about my family and our hardship. They allowed me to work whatever hours I could manage, which usually amounted to, at maximum, three hours a day. Some days I did not even come in!

I was concerned that I would lose yet another job dealing with a family emergency. Especially since the contract I signed said that I received a certain number of days off per year. Anything beyond that required a pay cut. The contract was thrown out the window, as my bosses allowed me to do whatever were necessary to care for my family.

Everyday I am thankful for everything that they did for me. We live in hurricane alley and it is important for us to know who is willing to come back early or stay during the storm. Every single year, I have never had a problem with writing my name on that sheet. I will be there for them. They supported me when I needed it and it has created a loyalty in me that no one can take away. It is the proverbial cliché; "I would walk through fire for them."

My Best Boss Ever

Because of their willingness to help me in a time of need, I never think of whether the tasks I am completing are in my job description. I do what is needed because they let me do what I needed to do in my time of need.

Clear the Way

*"Remember when life's path is steep to
keep your mind even."*
Horace (65 BC - 8 BC)

I am the sales representative of a large company that handles highly complex contracts. My boss understands the difficulty and clears the way for me to succeed.

Last month I had a client finally agree to a contract that I had been working on for three months. After the contract went back and forth, we finally agreed to terms. After reading it before signing, I noticed their request on billing. I knew the operations department would have a challenge with the request, and was worried that we would end up losing the sale on something minuscule.

I walked into my boss's office and asked his opinion. His respect and influence with this company that he had been a part of for 30 years, never ceased to amaze me. Within five minutes of talking with the Vice-President of Operations, a solution was worked out. He clears the way for me and it is remarkable to watch him in action.

I have worked for other companies that allow issues to sink a deal. Like torpedoes to an engine room, it has cost me commissions and has harmed the sales goals of the company. However, my best boss has influence and respect that he carries in the company to prevent those torpedoes from ever reaching the hull.

As we spoke one day about our individual roles within the company, he explained his vision for himself. "I see my job as the center of a football team. My job is to give you the ball and clear the way so you can see down the field and make things happen. I have to give you the time and opportunity to complete the pass or give you a running lane. Our goal is to get the ball to the end zone, and do a Lambeau Leap—to have a feeling of success and accomplishment. Our job is not to say we were true to the company policy and end up missing the deal. Our CEO doesn't want excuses; he expects results and results we will deliver."

His influence and assistance are invaluable assets to me. I have learned, because of him, how to navigate bureaucracy and still get things done without damaging my reputation or the working relationships I have with others. He clears the way and that makes him my best boss ever!

Coach Employees

*"I hear and I forget.
I see and I remember.
I do and I understand."*

Chinese Proverb

My best boss had the great mantra, "Never say what they can say, never do what they can do."

He said, "Asking questions and listening are a manager's most powerful tools." He once told me, "If you ask, you can never say anything wrong. If you talk too much, you can put yourself in a position where the wrong thing pops out." Observing him, I saw that he always was asking questions. He did not do this to solely keep from saying the wrong thing; he did it because he cared. He was always asking, "How is this project going? Do you need any of my help?" He would allow us to describe our situation while he pulled up a seat and listened intently. He would even seek us out to ask our advice on certain situations.

He taught me that coaching means asking questions, not just gathering facts. He would hear an employee's solution and their feelings on the subject and he would see how he could work the new perspective into the master plan.

The second part of his advice was as strong as the first, "Never do what they can do." He would show us how to do a task and then would hop up and have us sit down and do it ourselves. I remember the first time he showed me how to use the computer system. He entered some orders so I knew the process, but then handed me a stack of ten and watched me input them to make sure I did it right. It was not intrusive; he was merely being there for me if I had any questions. He also complemented me on my ability to catch on so quickly and my accuracy in typing.

When I asked him one day to explain how he developed his mantra, he replied, "Our objective is to develop employees. Asking them questions challenges them to think harder and more broadly about issues. That enlarges their perspective and improves their reasoning skills. But more importantly, it allows them to buy into the whole process." By asking questions, the employee says it, not the manager. That way, the employee learns it.

In developing employees, you want to make sure that you ask questions, listen carefully, and remember my best boss's mantra 'never say what they can say, and never do what they can do.'

Pat on the Back
Monica Zabolotny

*"The only way most people recognize their limits is by
trespassing on them."*
Tom Morris

Renee Werth is the best "pat on the back" boss I
have ever had! I remember when she first started
working with us. I would send out a routine
information email to someone and I would
forward a copy to her. I would end up getting a
reply back that said, "Thanks so much for
handling this," or "Great job keeping on top of
this!"

As crazy as that sounds, it was a bit strange at
first. Mostly because I had never had a boss do
that before. Here we are, seven months later and
she is continuing to dish out praise, both via email
and verbally. A pat on the back goes such a long
way and makes you feel appreciated and valued.

One of the "Boys"

"I couldn't leave my three teammates. I'd feel lost."
Dan Wheldon

My best boss—Arthur Prensky—and I met in 1973. He was the chair of the department of pediatric neurology. I received a dual appointment with the department of social work and pediatric neurology. I interviewed with the department of social work, so I met him on my first day of work.

As I walked into the hospital, he was running around the floor yelling, "Where is my puppet?" As I watched this lunatic run around and yell at everything, a nurse quietly walked up to him and said, "Dr. Prensky, empty everything out of your pockets." The puppet was the second thing to fall out. I remember thinking, "My gosh, this is supposed to be the great man that everyone has been talking about at Harvard?" He appeared nothing short of a joke.

However, I soon realized why everyone knew and admired this great man. Once you were on his team, you became one of his "boys." I too experienced this feeling when I got into a fight with a neurosurgeon. He wanted me to discharge a man that was too sick to even be considered for discharge. I explained that and he began to become frustrated. At one point, he referred to me as an incompetent social worker. I fired back, calling him an incompetent neurosurgeon and adding that if he were not so incompetent, the man would have been walking out of the hospital by now healed and healthy. It was, to be honest, completely inappropriate—especially for a 24-year-old social worker. However, Arthur backed me.

Arthur's love and devotion went farther than that. My father had passed away by the time that my husband proposed to me. At the time, Arthur offered his gigantic 9,000 square foot home to us for our wedding. We ended up having it somewhere else, but that offer was not out of the ordinary for one of Arthur's "boys."

He is now 78 years old and has recently dealt with the death of his wife. However, for individuals like Arthur, you are never truly alone. I have not worked for him for years, but even now, I am the executor of his living will, and I am honored to do it. It is the love, the devotion, and the loyalty that he held for each of his "boys" that made lifelong friendships out of his employees.

Make Them Look Like an Expert

"Expert: a man who makes three correct guesses consecutively."
Dr. Laurence J. Peter

I have had many good bosses, so when I say he is the best boss ever, it means a lot; but I am getting ahead of myself.

When I was brought onboard as a trainer, they had had a bad record with the position. In fact, in the interview I was told that if it did not work this time, that they were probably doing away with the position. However, that did not make Keith McDonald control me—that would have been the easy approach. He showed me his trust and respect in managing the position.

After I got a feel for the company and the lay of the land, he allowed me to run things the way I wanted to run them. In a previous company that I worked for, they handed me a training book and told me the date, time, and content of my training sessions. Here I was given free reign to see a need and choose to train on it. Even with this open-ended approach, I was given full support. In fact, Keith would even tell me, "You're the expert." That one sentence says volumes for the ideas and philosophies he held.

I like to open all of my training sessions by saying that what happens or is said in this session, stays in this session. Often times, I would discover

Human Resource problems, such as, "my manager is doing this," or "this is happening like this." This presented an ethical dilemma for me. I obviously was not going to run to their boss and complain that they were not doing things the right way, because that would break down the confidentiality circle thereby destroying any credibility I had.

Instead, I was able to go to Keith, who was also the director of human resources, and explain the problem without names and get his perspective. I could find out what he would do, and then go back to the employee and say, "What if you tried this." The employee needs to address the issue and this process allowed me to give them those needed skills. With this approach, everyone wins.

He lets me use his expertise so I that can even look more like an expert.

Don't You Suppose?

At my old bank, an ATM machine was in the middle of the lobby. When we reloaded the machine with new cash, it was supposed to be done with dual control. Two people were supposed to be there to work on the machine at the same time. We never really followed that protocol because of the machine's location. We always felt that since it was in the middle of the lobby that it was under more than dual control.

Like any branch, we soon got a new manager. There was an employee out there working on the machine by himself one day. To be honest, I thought nothing of it. My boss quietly walked over to me and looked around. She then bent down into my ear and whispered, "Don't you suppose you should be out there helping him?" It was a great subtle response, especially since she was new and could have caused all kinds of problems. I never felt threatened or yelled at, it was just a friendly reminder that I should get out of my chair and go help him.

New managers often have the mantra, "We're going to do it my way now." To be honest, rarely does that work. However, her effective whisper was all that was needed to correct a problem that had existed for years.

Integrity and a Catalyst for Change
Karen Morgan

"There is no such thing as a minor lapse of integrity."
                                        Tom Peters

I worked for my best boss two separate times. He possessed all the traits that I feel a best boss should have. He was a leader, interested in his employees, and did not micromanage. However, he possessed something that none of my other bosses have had; he put the company's best interests ahead of his own personal gains.

In fact, one of the times, I had the pleasure of working with him; he was leading the company through a merger. Through the whole process, he never let anyone discuss or question his future in the new corporation. He did not want to be viewed as doing something for his own self-interests instead of what was good for the company.

He would never entertain any questions about it, especially when the future structure was on the table. After the merger was complete, he was offered a position in the new company. I remember him taking a few days to decide what he wanted to do, and ended up deciding to move on and try something new.

His ability to see his role as doing what was best for the organization and not his own personal gain or motivation made him my best boss ever.

121

The other time that I worked for my best boss, I was working as a consultant for the company. In this instance, I had the pleasure to see his best leadership skills blossom. At the time, I was consulting for about 20 hours a week. In essence, I was an outsourced Vice-President of Marketing. He was always soft-spoken on the phone and let me decide when was best to come in or hold a meeting. One day, that all changed and he was abruptly different.

I received a call from him that very firmly said what time I should be at a meeting later that day. There was no small talk; there was no friendly laugh. It was very uncharacteristic of him. As I entered the room that afternoon, I was sitting among all of the senior managers. We all sat and looked at each other.

My best boss walked in and began to explain, "I am very disappointment that we have become careless and laissez-faire—including myself—with regards to expense management." He explained that we all had the ability to make a difference, but he did not understand why we seemingly did not want to. He said he called us all together so that we could spend the next two hours discovering and implementing a plan a fix the problem. Just as quickly as he entered, he turned around and left!

I sat stunned. My first gut reaction was, "The nerve!" My second thought was to remember whom I was dealing with. This compassionate, caring man wanted nothing more than the best for the organization. I pushed my initial anger aside and set out to help the rest of the team fix the problem. In only an hour, we had created a program that was sure to fix the challenge.

Later that night I thought about and explored why he acted the way that he did. I began to see that he was concerned with the direction of the corporation and he felt that to do more of the same was not going to change the paradigm. He was looking only at what was best for the company and took an uncharacteristic approach to gain everyone's attention. It was not that he did not trust us, because he left us alone to fix it ourselves! He understood that he needed to refocus us on something that needed our attention.

Sometimes to be a catalyst for change, you have to do something that is designed to change people's thinking. That is exactly what he did.

Vision
Mira Ness

"Leadership is the capacity to translate vision into reality."
Warren G. Bennis

My best boss is now the CEO of a financial institution, but he started at the bottom and worked his way up to. One of his greatest traits is that he never raises his voice, but his best trait is that he always smiles. His smile is infectious and it makes him very approachable.

His vision is one of his strongest characteristics. It is very important to have vision. The City of New York was selling a building for $1 in Yonkers, NY, and Jeff had his institution purchase it and renovated it for low-income housing. Many actors qualify for housing in the complex. The project, when it was completed, had 18 apartments available for actors. It was a successful renovation project. Everyone told him not to do it, but he just kept pushing on. Now the building is alive with many creative tenants. The building stands as a testament to his character and persistence.

He is my best boss because he takes a project and sees it to completion. He has a great way of getting everyone behind his vision.

He is also a big believer in weekly staff meetings to continually sell the vision and to build a stronger team. For example, it took us several months for all employees to go over the book

124

"NUTS," which is about Southwest Airlines. He liked the culture of Southwest Airlines, and so he thought, why not share that with the staff. That booked helped us determine how we would change our corporate culture.

He was a believer in lifelong learning. Having everyone get together to review the book, "NUTS" was an excellent way to show his commitment to lifelong learning.

Winning Presentations

"To win without risk is to triumph without glory."
Pierre Corneille

I had given presentations before, but never one this important. I knew if I were successful in making a strong case for the project, the company would benefit greatly. Of course, I also knew that if my presentation were successful I would benefit greatly as well. I wanted to be persuasive and different. I had attended far too many presentations that relied so heavily on PowerPoint that people were lost, distracted or bored.

Tons of PowerPoint slides were the norm, but my instincts told me that was not the best answer. As I thought about my situation, my thoughts came to the Vice President. I had long been a fan of her presentations and wondered if maybe she could give me some pointers. I was nervous to ask for her help, but this was a very important presentation, so I sent her an email.

I was pleasantly surprised to find that she would be willing to help me even though her schedule was full; she could make some time for a brief conversation.

I opened the meeting by thanking Jayne for her time and telling her again, why I admired her presentations so much. After we got past these pleasantries, Jayne said she had seven things she always did when creating a presentation. As I prepared to take notes she said, "First, let me warn you that not all of these ideas are directly about PowerPoint, but all of them will help your presentation be more successful and you'll avoid death by PowerPoint."

I smiled, as I had not heard the phrase "Death by PowerPoint" before, but I had certainly experienced it.

Then Jayne handed me a list she had photocopied with the seven tips on it. As we discussed the list, I added the notes included below.

Seven Ways to Avoid Death by PowerPoint

Think about the audience. If you want to persuade someone, the most important thing is to think first, about whom they are, what their concerns are and to better understand their perspective. Start planning for any presentation by starting with your audience.

Think about your message. Once you begin to understand the audience, then think about your message. What are your key points? What is your audience's perspective on your message? What details might not be necessary for or make sense to your audience? Remember, your message is probably clear to you, but this may be the first time your audience is even thinking about this topic. Help make it clear for them too.

Think about the action you want the audience to take. Ultimately your presentation is about what happens because of what you say. Make sure you clearly understand what actions you want your audience to take and make sure your presentation helps and persuades them to take those next steps.

Use fewer slides. The presenter using too many slides filled with too much information often causes "Death by PowerPoint." Though every presentation is different, chances are good that you can cut the number of your current slides in half and double the effectiveness of your talk.

Use fewer words. After you cut the number of slides, reduce the number of words on each slide. Unless it is a definition or a statement needed verbatim, do not include any sentences. Also, try to keep your bullet points to four words or less.

Use fewer bells and whistles. Just because the program gives you 100 different fonts, sounds and animation options it does not mean you need to use them (all). Remember that PowerPoint is meant to be a visual aid, not to be the show or to get in the way of your message. Less is almost always more.

Use more visuals. Cut the words and augment your message with pictures and other visual cues. They will be more memorable and will help keep your audience engaged and tracking with you.

Stop thinking about the PowerPoint first. It is not about the slides; it is about the people, the messages and the actions you want them to take.

As I reviewed the list, I mentioned to Jayne that there were eight items on her list of seven ways. She said, "The last one is really the most important one. When we think about our slides first we will create the presentation from the slides rather than creating a presentation and supporting it with a few slides. Besides, no one ever accused me of being an accountant." She smiled as I thanked her.

As I walked out the door, she said, "Don't thank me now, thank me by using these ideas and wowing the group with your presentation."

Of course, I followed her advice and created a few slides to support my key messages. The presentation went great and the first email I received after the project moved forward was from Jayne. She said she was proud of me and that she looked forward to seeing many more presentations in the future.

My Favorite Manager

On a plane one day—and I am on them often—a man gave me some questions he had written down about a best boss he had. He said he used these questions to help focus on being the best boss he could be. He had heard a quote from Anthony Robbins: "Successful people mirror, match and model success." Therefore, with that thought he decided to write down some questions on how his best boss would handle a situation.

He said, "Think of the best boss you ever had. To model the behavior of your best bosses you can ask these questions."

To improve teamwork this manager will ___.

When faced with adversity this manager will ___.

When explaining a concept this manager will ___.

To keep control of an unruly group this manager will ___.

To reinforce important behavior this manager will ___.

Employees respect this manager because ___.

Rory Rowland

Believe in Each Other

*"One of the greatest of all principles
is that man can do
what they think they can do."*
Norman Vincent Peale

A coworker broke her arm playing softball. She was rushed to the emergency room and found out that physical therapy and six weeks out of work was necessary. Ouch.

At work my best boss pulled us all in together to explain the circumstances and explained that we would have to cover her workload. I had worked for other bosses when I had to cover the workload of my coworkers. To them it resulted in dumping all of the work on one person—the first person in eyeshot got it. It taught me if someone called in sick avoid eye contact. With my best boss, it was different.

He held team meetings in the morning so that the important tasks could be divided up between all of us. He constantly found the time to walk around and compliment us for our success of getting her work done on time. We covered so well that we kept our record at being the top performing office in the whole company three months in a row. My coworker was so pleased that she did not have to catch up when she got back and everyone slowly started to turn over work to her so that she could get back into the groove. It was an amazing team building exercise that we soon realized that we

131

could accomplish anything together. My boss inspired us to do more with less, which is a challenge that many organizations face.

Without his leadership, we never would have even attempted to cover the workload of another employee without outside help. However, with him, we never had to ask for help. People will always rally around a cause they believe in, and my best boss helped us believe in each other.

Respect Performance

I went into my best boss's office one day with a question. I could see him sitting behind his desk, visibly upset. Having always had a good relationship with him, I asked what was wrong. He replied that he had sent a proposal to upper management to get a raise for our department. Senior managers shot it down.

There was a pause and remorse came over him. He requested that I not discuss the details of our conversation, and that it had been inappropriate of him to discuss it with me. I respected his wishes, then asked my question, and left. I did not share our conversation with anyone.

A few weeks later, he called a meeting with our entire department. He explained that he had noticed our excellent performance last quarter and wanted to reward us. He said that the upper management had just installed a bonus plan for superior performance. He did not even take all the credit even though I knew it was his idea. If we increased the sales figures from last year by at least 10 percent, we could get a bonus. The more we increased sales, the bigger the bonus!

He fought for all of us and we had no trouble hitting the goal. He actively fought upper management on our behalf, and that is what made him my best boss ever. I would be willing to shovel behind the elephants in the circus if it meant I worked for him, simply because of his respect for my work and my opinion.

The other thing I respected was the fact that he did not cut down senior management. He could have come back from that initial meeting and destroyed senior management in our eyes. I have seen managers verbally smear the up line mangers. Those kinds of managers always complain about the 'ivory tower.' He did not do that. He kept the respect of senior management, even though he disagreed, but he also fought for us. It was a win-win all around. If I ever become a manager, I will not cut down senior management with my employees.

Appreciation

*"By appreciation, we make excellence in others
our own property."*

Voltaire

We were having renovations completed in our office and a new bathroom was installed. A plumber forgot to tighten a fitting in the upstairs bathroom and water leaked all weekend! To say the least, we had a flood. We had to file a claim against the plumber's insurance company, and since we had all chipped in to help, the settlement was more than enough to fix the damage. To demonstrate his appreciation for extra time and effort everyone put into the office during the crisis, my boss gave everyone gift certificates! We received a massage package or a gift card and dinner for two at *the* exclusive restaurant in town. Never before had I had a boss actually give a windfall to their staff, especially that nice of one. Of course, verbal praise is nice, but the tangible benefits that my boss provided were something that will always make him my best boss.

Change Direction

"The art of progress is to preserve order amid change."
Alfred North Whitehead

She always told me to treat others as you would like to be treated, and to be honest, even when it is painful. She was always skilled socially and knew just when an employee needed the truth. It was at that time that her greatest skill, coaching, took center stage. It was on one of those days that I needed honesty, that she coached me in the direction that I needed to go with my life.

I was feeling worthless at work. I would come in, do my job, and go home. I did not really feel challenged and I never felt like my talents were being utilized. In the past I had approached bosses about how I felt, that I did not think I was using my full potential, but was always brushed away. I felt like I was being a nuisance for even suggesting I had bigger plans in the company, or my life. Therefore, I approached my best boss and mustered up the courage to say, "I am not being challenged."

Right away, the coaching conversation with her was different than my other bosses. She listened and really attempted to hear me.

I told her, "I am just not happy working here anymore." Other bosses have told me at this point, 'there are other places to work.' However, that was not the issue, I would not have been

136

happy anywhere with the malaise that I was feeling.

She replied, "What do you mean not happy?"

"I'm just sort of bored and I feel like the work I do doesn't make much of a difference."

"Now we're getting somewhere," she replied. "You're bored. So what do you want?"

"I want to feel like my talents are being used and that my work means something. I don't know if that's possible in my current position."

She smiled and said, "What do you think is possible or impossible?"

That was a good question, it made me pause, and I left her office after that to resume my internal dialogue.

That question made me think. What is possible? What is impossible? Why do I think it is impossible? I began to re-evaluate everything I had ever thought about the concept of 'impossibility.'

A few weeks later she asked, "Is going back to school was impossible?" I always thought it was, but now I wondered if that was true. She helped me work out a game plan to do some different projects in the office and take on more responsibility. That helped my current boredom and lack of challenge. She went further and helped me even more with the challenge of going back to school with two kids and a husband.

It took me eight years to complete my degree part time. After I graduated, I got a great promotion in the company. They had a policy you had to have a college degree to be in management and I am now in a position where I know that everyday I am going to be challenged and I make a difference. I will never forget her coaching that day. She listened to me at a level that I would never experience at work. Because of her honesty, I changed the direction of my life for the better. Many bosses would have blown me off as soon as I said, "I am just not happy working here anymore."

Build Relationships

"Treat people as if they were what they ought to be and you help them become what they are capable of being."
Johann Wolfgang von Geothe

My best boss would always say, "Make a sale, make a living. Make a relationship, create a life." His belief was that relationships were the foundation to life, both professional and personal.

He always said his famous line with a Cheshire cat smile, "No one ever wished they had a smaller network."

He was amazing at giving us time to develop relationships with our clients. One circumstance really stands out in my mind.

I was brand new to the sales world at the time. Senior management had just had a 'rah-rah' full day meeting at a hotel with this hot shot 'professional speaker.' We had to do role-playing (oh how I love to role play) on how to get in and out of a potential client's office in less than 17 minutes. The speaker's technique was to get in and out fast. They taught us to ask for the close early. They said, "Earlier is better than later, and it beats never asking, every time." I went home that night and memorized my open, hook'em and closing techniques from the three-ring binder they gave us. This was a sales strategy that others in the company had used with success. I thought, 'why re-invent the wheel?' They kept telling us, selling is a numbers game, see more potential clients, and you will make more sales. I visited quadruple my normal number over the next week but sold less than half my norm. I was devastated.

When I walked into the office, my boss saw the disappointment on my face and quickly asked me what was wrong. I told him, "I memorized all the sales stuff senior managers told us, and saw four times the normal number of people, and made half of the sales. I told him, "This sucks." He said, "Come here."

We went into his office and he showed me his old beat up note cards. He had all these 3 x 5 cards with client's names and personal information on them. I thought to myself, I feel like those things look. He said, "You see all these names in here? These are clients who I still play golf with all the time. These are my professional friends. He told me, "Make the sale, you make a living. But, make a relationship, and you make a life." He said, "My goal is to make friends, and build relationships. Friends buy from friends. The other departments can sell that way because they sell 'wam bam' stuff we sell repeat order items that require relationships. Success on our side of the company requires building trust, and building relationships. It will take time, but work on building relationships."

The next day I went out with his strategy in mind. I did not have an entrance, open, hook'em or close approach. I went out to build trust and make friends. I visited four clients that day—four. However, I walked away, wrote down their kid's names, their birthdays, and their favorite hobbies, anything personal they said, I remembered and wrote down. My database of friends began to grow over time. Additionally, over the next few months, my sales began to grow, and within the year, it was double my performance from last year. My best boss understood the power of building relationships and allowed me the freedom to create those relationships without fear of losing my job.

Never Eat Lunch Alone

My boss was always trying to find someone to eat lunch with him. Our clients, employees, and even the janitors were his lunch partners. He did not always buy, but he took a sincere interest in us and listened to anything that was on our minds.

I once asked him why he was always trying to eat with someone. Why not just enjoy a nice quiet lunch alone? He replied that he had read the book, "Never Eat Lunch Alone" by Keith Ferrazzi and was hooked on the idea. He said he immediately noticed the huge difference it made in the relationships he had with his clients and employees. He also leaned in and said, "I am really learning about what is going on, it is a great tool to help me manage the office." He was always a vivacious and fun guy, it was easy for him to get people to go to lunch with him. Therefore, his technique of never going to lunch alone, and the lessons it taught me, created a very successful boss out of him, and a great successor out of me.

Avoid the Heart Attack

"Action may not always bring happiness, but there is no happiness without action."
Benjamin Disraeli

I never fully understood how great my best boss was until I became a boss. I was faced with the decision of terminating an employee. I remembered that my boss had hesitated with the very same problem a few years before I was promoted, so I went to seek his advice.

He shared some very valuable information.

I asked when he knew if he should fire someone or not. He replied, "When you think about firing them more than coaching. I hated terminating people, but when I started to think about firing them more than trying to coach them, I knew I had hit the tipping point."

"But how do you do it?"

"Before I fired my first employee and your former colleague, I read a few books on firing employees. Two main ideas stood out. Sometimes managers care more about the employee's job than the employee does. This idea was a real revelation for me, simply because I cared more about her staying than she did. The other idea I learned was that it is the people that you do not fire that give you the heart attack; not the ones you do. I

143

realized that I was doing more damage by keeping her around."

He also offered advice that I found very useful. "Do it fast and have a prepared statement reviewed by an attorney. After you have their final check printed, make sure you have a human resource representative in the room. When you are done reading the statement, leave and let HR take over. Never get into a discussion with an employee; they should be aware before this moment why this is happening. No need to discuss it further. The best firing is when an employee walks in to the conference room and says, 'I think I know why I am here.' That statement by the employee demonstrates they were well informed of the performance requirements."

Although I did not understand the struggle he went through to protect the company and us until I was a manager myself, I now understand that he was my best boss ever.

Shine and Glow

"What's given shines, What's received is rusty."
Benjamin Franklin

His heart attack changed everything. He used to control probably half of the workload of the entire office. After his heart attack, he called me into his office to discuss his future with the department. He explained that he could not pull 11-hour days anymore and that he had typed up a list of things that he had to have accomplished on a monthly basis. It was good the heart attack taught him what we used to grumble about. He never really delegated, and it drove everyone in the office nuts. Why have us on the payroll if he was going to do it all?

I had no idea that we could do this much more for him! The heart attack taught him how to delegate.

Of course, I was more than happy to step up to the plate and help out, and I took over many of his high profile tasks. He called everyone into his office that day, explained the same thing, and gave away some tasks so that he could get his workload down to a manageable level.

He set up a time each month to review our progress to make sure that we were still on track. His willingness to hand over tasks he could no longer handle made him my best boss. A heart attack is a difficult way to learn to delegate, but I guess it was better than the alternative.

145

His delegation of tasks also made us look more promising in the eyes of the senior management, which really helped my career! He came up with a phrase for it. He would smile and say, "You all can shine and I can glow." He knew his days of shining were over, but he was more than willing to sit back and glow while we all started to really shine.

Roundtable

My best boss ever was the CEO of the company. I did not work directly for him, but he had weekly roundtables with employees. About 10 or 12 people from different departments would receive an invitation, and he would sit down and answer any questions that they asked. Overtime we became more open and were not afraid to ask any business question. It was great to have the opportunity to be invited that week, but even if you were not, he invited those who did attend to discuss everything with everyone. In addition, believe me, everyone would ask those attendees about any new details. They even started having a person who attended take notes and then put them on the intranet for everyone to review, it became a running log of what was happening in the company.

The employees that did attend were like moths drawn into the flame. He was a funny and easygoing guy that really knew his stuff. It was a great way for all of us to learn about the company. His strategy to climb down from the mountaintop and discuss business issues with employees made him my best boss, even though he was the CEO.

Best Boss
Steven Caporale

"The best way to predict the future is to invent it."
Alan Kay

In my 20-year career, I have worked with dozens of managers. I have only had two bosses I would consider best. I guess that speaks poorly about management skills and leadership in the United States. However, one boss had the greatest influence on me. I strive to incorporate his management techniques in my day-to-day work life.

The boss was Steve Hood. When I worked for him, he was a senior vice president at a national development company and I was a project manager working on his team. I spent two years with Steve–in numerous assignments, and in many high-pressure and time sensitive environments. One project was so intense it is the closest I have ever come to a nervous breakdown.

Steve was a boss who expected high-performance and engagement from those who worked for him. His assumption was that you would always give your best, and because of that expectation–and the respect we had for Steve, everyone on the team strived to give their best at all times. Steve was consistently (which is where most bosses falter) encouraging, motivating and, more than all, empathetic to those he worked with. The teams we had under Steve were also the best

148

teams I ever worked on. They were like ensembles of great jazz musicians; we knew our part, there was no politics and we ran like a precision machine.

Steve was the same with those he met. Five minutes with Steve and you knew he cared about you. It was his gift. Whether he was talking to an employee, a contractor he just met, or a clerk at Starbucks. He would commend strangers (gas station employees, restaurant workers, day laborers) on a job well done and encourage them to better their skills and give 100 percent, as it will open additional doors.

Steve never tried to "hold people down" like some bosses do. He encouraged those at every level and division of the organization to get as much education as possible and always work to improve one's profession. He was not intimidated that those below him rose up to be more successful and in higher positions. He considered it an honor. Steve has likely brought out the best in hundreds of employees over his 35-year career. I know this because of the relationship he has with people who still call him. Steve always has several former employees who are now multi-millionaires and they still keep in touch with him. He had this affect on me and on most people he worked with. Years later, I still talk about Steve with people who have worked with him, and the sentiment and recollection are similar to what I express in this writing. Steve genuinely cared for people. That trait makes him my best boss ever.

After September 11th, the development company had a large number of lay-offs, including me, and I learned as I was being terminated that it hurt Steve as much as it hurt me. He stood tall to higher-ups to get me a fair severance package and walked me out of the building, not because he had to, because he wanted to.

Looking back, Steve never uttered a malicious word about someone else and treated everyone, of all social status, equally. He inspired loyalty and was a master at building people's confidence and empowering them to do better than they even knew they could. We could all learn a lot from a boss like Steve.

Know Your Material
Roy Crawford

While I was working at Fort Lewis, Colin Powell was appointed to his 4th Star, making him one of my bosses. He decided to make a visit out to Fort Lewis. Many people at the time thought that he was too political and did not deserve his 4th or even his 3rd Star. He showed up to the base and just blew everybody away.

He attended our staff meetings and he was versed on every training exercise or weapon's training that we were having. He knew the objectives we held and could talk tough about everything. People thought he was all politics, but soon realized that you could not underestimate the man who would soon become our Secretary of State.

The lesson it taught me was to be an excellent leader; know your stuff. It also taught me never to underestimate someone before I met him or her.

151

Lifelong Learning

"Play is the beginning of knowledge."

George Dorsey

My best boss ever was committed to lifelong learning.

Every year at our annual departmental dinner, he would give out the 'Lifelong Learner Award.' Everyone in our department voted for the selection of the Lifelong Learner Award. His commitment focused everyone on continuing our education and self-paced learning.

My best boss always was always reading a book or listening to an audio program in his car. He had a huge library in his office and he lead by example.

Lifelong learning is a critically important component of success for any person working today.

What did it do for me? I had my college degree in business and I went back to school part-time and got my master's degree. To top it off, the year I graduated I earned the Lifelong Learner Award. I am no longer with that company, but it helped me focus on lifelong learning goals and helped me have the confidence to apply for my current job.

37 Things People Learned

At the conclusion of my seminars, I ask people what they learned from the session. They write it down as our final top 10-list exercise. Here is a compilation of the things people wrote down at the conclusion of the seminars.

1. Be big enough to accept responsibility for the team. Real leaders take the blame.

2. Give credit to others—if you do not, you will never earn their respect.

3. Always sell the dream of your team—where are we going? What are our hopes and aspirations?

4. Your job is to make the organization look good. Your job is to help others succeed.

5. Coach your people to success; tell them they will not fail you as long as they stay in the game. (Assuming of course they have the talent and skills to do the job.)

6. Show your leadership by taking action; have an action orientation.

7. Become an "Obnoxious Optimist." Always be optimistic.

8. Negatives up and positives down. (Never complain to your employees, it makes you look petty and small. Complain to someone higher up, compliment down to your employees.)

9. Compliment your people with the 5 S's compliment rule (page 45)

10. Be a lifelong learner and encourage your people to be lifelong learners. The more you learn the more you earn. Make a traveling university.

11. Prepare everyone to take over your job. (Leave a legacy)

12. Ask your customers what they think. They will tell you the truth.

13. Ask your people for their opinion. They will tell you if they trust you and if they do not, then you know where to start building your team.

14. Common sense and good judgment need to be your guide.

15. MBWA. If people do not want to see you, or you do not want to see them, you are already in trouble. (MBWA = management by wandering around.)

16. Know and express your principles of management by working in the organization.

17. Create service standards. If you do not have one, look up Ritz Carlton's Service Standards.

18. Never be afraid to say, "I made a mistake." People know, get over it.

19. Decorate your language with praise.

20. Celebrate accomplishments. When you accomplish something, get excited and get everyone excited.

21. Do you take employees to lunch? Why not?

22. Do you have integrity? If not, do not manage people.

23. Be a backstop. Back them up, if you want them to back you up.

24. Ask what did you learn this week and what can we do better?

25. Question the information from your sources from time to time. You might be surprised at what they are not telling you.
26. Become curious about everything. Keep asking questions.

27. After asking many questions, shut up. Listen.

28. Ask the hard questions no one else is. Like, "What are your expectations?" and "What is the reason we are doing _____?"

29. Use silence as a tool. Sometimes it is just a matter of waiting and listening.

30. Practice brevity. Ask them what they learned.

31. Be specific when singing the praises of your employee(s) or team (s). If you say only, "good job" you should be fired. Tell them what they did right.

32. "Successful people make a conscious decision on a daily basis toward improvement" –Anthony Robbins.

33. Ask forgiveness rather than permission from time to time. It shows character, judgment and belief in you. Just be prepared to demonstrate the effectiveness of what you did.

34. Give a dollar to anyone who can restate the Mission and service standards statement. Give him or her $20 if they can do it backwards.

35. Never let the customer see how you run your circus. They do not need to know.

36. Recognize that Leadership and Management are two different things.

37. Have compassion. Sometimes, you are all the person in front of you has and they are looking to you for answers.

38. Do not do worker's work. Let them do it. Show them, teach them, coach them and let them.

39. Be willing to jump in and lend a hand when needed, just not all of the time.

40. Go the extra mile, under promise and over deliver—yes, I know, I said there would be 37; I just wanted to go the extra mile.

Characteristics of the Best Boss

Focus on strengths
Opportunities to grow
Taught to pay attention
Believed in me
Would back me up
Encouraged employees
Friendly
Considerate
Fearless
Confident
Supporter
Empowering
Trust
Stretched beyond my
   comfort
Cares about your
   viewpoint
Respect
Teacher / mentor
Empowered
Gave confidence
Humility
Willing to accept
   mistakes
Showed respect
Approachable
Trustworthy
Challenged others
Humorous
Good communicator
Made other feel
   important

Recognized talent

Go get what you want—
   don't sit back
Allow us to participate
Encouraging
Praise
Caring
Positive attitude
Strict
Passionate
Makes you smile
Prankster
Influential
Attention
Compassionate
Sounding board
Good coach
Saw potential
Threw title out the
   window
Worked side by side
   with employees
Humorous
Positive
Optimistic
Showed interest in
   personal life
Invested in growth
Teacher
Modeled behavior
Training
Focused on strengths

Quick Order Form

To Fax: 816-350-7773

To Telephone: 816-478-3249

To Email: rrr3@ix.netcom.com

To Mail: Rory Rowland
       14401 Covington Rd.
       Independence, MO 64055

Please send me more copies of "My Best Boss Ever" $19.95 each and $3.99 for shipping and handling. Please call for quantity discounts. I understand that these orders come with a lifetime guarantee. If you're not happy, Rory's not happy.

_____

_____

_____

Please send me FREE information on:

☐ Books ☐ Speaking ☐ Consulting

Name: _____

Address: _____

City: _____ State: _____ Zip: _____

Telephone:_____

Email Address:_____

My Best Boss Ever

Quick Order Form

To Fax: 816-350-7773

To Telephone: 816-478-3249

To Email: rrr3@ix.netcom.com

To Mail: Rory Rowland
14401 Covington Rd.
Independence, MO 64055

Please send me more copies of "My Best Boss Ever" $19.95 each and $3.99 for shipping and handling. Please call for quantity discounts. I understand that these orders come with a lifetime guarantee. If you're not happy, Rory's not happy.

_____

_____

_____

Please send me FREE information on:

☐ Books   ☐ Speaking   ☐ Consulting

Name: _____

Address: _____

City: _____ State: _____ Zip: _____

Telephone:_____

Email Address:_____